Hélène Le Berre

Liberty
cross stitch

24 designs to sew

SEARCH PRESS

✤ Contents

1. Just for you

 Floral bag

Size:
35 × 35cm (13¾ × 13¾in) plus the handles
Materials:
Two 34 × 17cm (13½ × 6¾in) pieces of 28-count (11 threads/cm) ivory linen, DMC
ref. 3865 • 115 × 55cm (45¼ × 21¾in) rectangle of Liberty Tana Lawn (Enfield)
• DMC Special Mouliné stranded cotton: two skeins of shade 598 and one skein
each of shades 760 and 370 • 85 × 30cm (33½ × 11¾in) rectangle of wadding (batting)
• Two 30 × 13cm (11¾ × 5in) rectangles of stiff interfacing • pair of leather handles,
roughly 45cm (17¾in) long • repositionable fabric adhesive spray • sewing thread
to match the fabric • sewing machine • sewing kit • fabric marker pen.
Refer to the chart on page 72 and the patterns on pages 92–93.

EMBROIDERY

Work the design on each rectangle of linen, positioning the embroidery so that the red reference mark (bottom-right of the chart) is 2cm (¾in) from the right side and lower edge of the fabric. Work each cross stitch over two linen threads using two strands of Special Mouliné cotton. Work the stamens in backstitch using two strands of embroidery cotton.

STITCHING THE FABRIC

1 Checking the direction of the print, transfer patterns A and B to the wrong side of the Liberty fabric twice (transfer the reference marks on pattern A also). Cut out, adding 1cm (⅜in) seam allowances all round.
2 Spray glue on to the wrong side of the two bag pieces A and attach the wadding. Trim the wadding to match the fabric.
3 Quilt the padded fabric by stitching along the vertical pattern lines.
4 On each bag piece A, fold each point X' over to X in the centre, right sides together, to make pleats. Stitch just inside the fabric edge to hold the pleats in place.
5 Overlay the two bag pieces (A), right sides together. Pin, then stitch the sides and base 1cm (⅜in) from the edge, leaving 3cm (1¼in) open at the top of each side. Turn right side out.
6 Join the two lining pieces (B) in the same way.
7 Place the lining in the bag, wrong sides together. Pin the top of the lining to the top of the bag and then stitch the top edge, taking a 5mm (¼in) seam allowance. Carefully sew the lining to the bag at the side slits using slip stitch.

ATTACHING THE EMBROIDERED BORDERS

1 Spray glue on to one side of each rectangle of interfacing. Centre an embroidered fabric rectangle on top, making sure the embroidery is nicely positioned on the right side. Fold the excess fabric over the interfacing and attach it to the back with large slip stitches, taking care not to go through to the right side of the embroidery.
2 From the remaining Liberty fabric cut two 32 × 15cm (12½ × 6in) rectangles to line the embroidery and four 6cm (2¼in) squares. These squares will be used to attach the bag handles. Fold each square in half, right sides together and stitch the long side 1cm (⅜in) from the edge. Turn the tabs obtained right side out, slip them into the loops of the handles and fold in half.
3 Centre one rectangle of fabric on the back of each embroidery and crease where the edges overlap the embroidery. Fold the fabric edges along the creased lines or just inside them and glue these seam allowances down. Apply glue to the back of the whole piece and stick it to the back of the embroidery. Carefully adjust the turn-ins level with the edges or fractionally inside them. Complete the remaining stages before the glue dries.
4 Slip the ends of the bag tabs under the fabric of the embroidered borders, leaving a space of 16cm (6¼in) between them, and pin in place.
5 Slip the top of the fabric bag between the linen and fabric along the bottom edge by 1cm (⅜in). Sew with slip stitch across all the layers. Sew the upper edge and the sides of the fabric using slip stitch, strengthening the stitching where the tabs of the handles go.

TIPS
CUT YOUR PATTERNS OUT OF ACETATE SHEETS, AVAILABLE FROM CRAFT AND QUILTING SUPPLIERS, SO THAT YOU CAN USE THEM AGAIN AND AGAIN. FOR THIS PATTERN, YOU WILL NEED 40 × 25cm (15¾ × 9¾IN).
TO TRANSFER THE FOLD MARKS X AND X', CUT LITTLE V-SHAPED NOTCHES IN THE SEAM ALLOWANCE.

✳ Pocket mirror

Size:
8cm (3¼in) diameter

Materials:
8cm (3¼in) mirror • 15cm (6in) square of 28-count (11 threads/cm) mauve linen, DMC, ref. 3743 • 20 × 10cm (7¾ × 4in) piece of Liberty Carnaby Jersey (Venus Leaf) or another stretchy fabric • DMC Special Mouliné stranded cotton: 1 skein of each colour listed in the chart key • 8cm (3¼in) diameter circle of stiff interfacing • 1cm (⅜in) ivory white plastic press stud • 7cm (2¾in) diameter circle of Bristol board • sewing thread to match the fabric • sewing kit • fabric marker pen • pair of compasses.
Refer to the chart on page 73.

EMBROIDERY

Embroider the motif in the centre of the linen, working each stitch over two linen threads. Use two strands of Special Mouliné cotton for the cross stitch and one strand for the backstitch.

SEWING AND ASSEMBLY

1 Cut one 9cm (3½in) circle from the fabric – leave space on the remaining fabric to cut a second circle later on (see step 5).

2 Centre the embroidery over the circle of interfacing and pin it in place. Trim the excess linen 1.5cm (⅝in) from the interfacing. Using a double length of thread, work running stitch all around the edge of the linen circle in the margin. Pull the thread to gather the linen down over the interfacing, and arrange the gathers neatly; fasten off. Sew the linen overlap to the interfacing using large slip stitches, taking care not to go through to the front of the embroidery.

3 Repeat the gathering process around the stiffened embroidery, this time working 5mm (¼in) from the edge. Place the circle of Bristol board on the wrong side of the fabric and pull the thread so the embroidery wraps around the board; do not fasten off the stitches yet. Iron the back of the embroidery to hold the shape then remove the Bristol board and fasten off the running stitch.

4 Pin the embroidery to the fabric, wrong sides together, and trim away any excess fabric neatly; sew around the edge using slip stitch.

5 Cut out an 8cm (3¼in) diameter circle from the remaining fabric (this dimension is justified because of the elasticity of the jersey). Turn in 5mm (¼in) all round the edge and press. Work running stitch around the circle as before, stitching close to the edge. Slip the mirror into the circle and pull the thread to tighten the fabric around it; fasten off the stitching securely.

6 Join the two circles by making a bar-tack hinge using Mouliné cotton 3713. Sew one part of the press stud to each circle, on the same axis as the bar so that when the mirror is closed the bar-tack hinge is on one side and the press studs meet on the other side.

❄ Hair accessory

Size:
8 × 8cm (3¼ × 3¼in)
Materials:
Fabric-covered hair band • 10cm (4in) square of 28-count (11 threads/cm) ivory linen, DMC ref. 3865 • 30 × 10cm (11¾ × 4in) piece of Liberty Tana Lawn (Mauvey) • DMC Special Mouliné stranded cotton: 1 skein of each colour listed in the chart key • 15 × 10cm (6 × 4in) piece of stiff interfacing • sewing thread to match the fabric • sewing kit • fabric marker pen • pair of compasses.
Refer to the chart on page 73.

EMBROIDERY
Embroider the motif in the centre of the linen, working each cross stitch over one linen thread and using one strand of Special Mouliné cotton.

MAKING UP
1 From the stiff interfacing, cut out one 5.5cm (2¼in) diameter circle, one 4cm (1½in) circle and one 3cm (1¼in) circle.
2 Centre the embroidered linen on the largest circle of interfacing and pin it in place. Trim the excess linen 1.5cm (⅝in) from the interfacing. Using a double length of thread, work running stitch all around the edge of the circle in the linen margin. Pull the thread to gather the linen down over the interfacing and then fasten off. Sew the linen overlap to the interfacing using large slip stitches, taking care not to go through to the right side of the embroidery.
3 Selecting two different areas of the fabric, cut out one 7cm (2¾in) circle and one 5cm (2in) circle. Working as before, gather the 7cm (2¾in) circle around the 4cm (1½in) circle of interfacing and the remaining fabric circle around the remaining interfacing circle.
4 Taking inspiration from the photographs shown here, fix the three circles to each other with a few strong stitches on the wrong side. Place the joined circles on the wrong side of the remaining fabric.

TIP
THIS PRETTY EMBROIDERY WOULD MAKE A WONDERFUL BADGE OR PATCH TO STITCH TO A GARMENT OR BACKPACK, AND YOU COULD DO THE SAME WITH THE FABRIC CIRCLES TOO. SIMPLY FOLLOW STEPS 1–3 ABOVE AND THEN SLIP STITCH THE COMPLETED CIRCLES TO YOUR CHOSEN GARMENT OR BAG.

5 Trace the general outline on to the fabric then cut out, adding a 1cm (⅜in) allowance all around. Snip the allowance in the corners and along the curves to make folding easier. Fold the allowance to the wrong side of the fabric and iron in place. Attach this piece to the back of the circles with slip stitch. Sew the assembly on to the hair band, 5.5cm (2¼in) from one end.

✿ Pretty bow

Length:
132cm (52in)
Materials:
10 × 137cm (4 × 54in) piece of 2-count (11 threads/cm) ivory linen, DMC, ref. 3865
• 7 × 134cm (2¾ × 52¾in) piece of Liberty Tana Lawn (Sarah's Secret Garden)
• DMC Special Mouliné stranded cotton: 1 skein of each colour listed in the chart
key • sewing thread to match the fabric • sewing kit • fabric marker pen.
Refer to the chart on page 81.

EMBROIDERY

Lay out the fabric with the short sides at the top and bottom.
Mark out the position of the first motif, centred 2.5cm (1in)
above the lower edge. Stitch the embroidery, working each
stitch over two threads of linen and using two strands of Special
Mouliné cotton for both the cross stitch and backstitch. Repeat
the pattern fourteen times in total from bottom to top.

SEWING

1 Fold over each long edge of the linen strip to meet in the
   middle, wrong sides together then fold over 2.5cm (1in) at
   each end to obtain a band 5 × 132cm (2 × 52in). Cut off the
   excess linen, 1cm (⅜in) from the folds.
2 Fold the four sides of the fabric over by 1cm (⅜in) to the
   wrong side to obtain a band 5 × 132cm (2 × 52in).
3 Pin the linen and fabric strips wrong sides together and slip
   stitch together all round.
4 Tie the band in a bow, forming two little loops and leaving
   two long tails. We stitched the bow to a fabric bag, but you
   can add it to whatever you like.

TIP
DO NOT WORRY IF YOU ARE UNABLE TO OBTAIN THE LIBERTY FABRIC
SPECIFIED ABOVE. USE ANY LIGHTWEIGHT COTTON OF YOUR CHOICE OR
EVEN RECYCLE FABRIC – THE FABRIC FROM A DUVET COVER, DRESS OR
SKIRT, FOR EXAMPLE. JUST MAKE SURE IT HAS A LIGHT, SUMMERY DESIGN
THAT WILL NOT SHOW THROUGH THE LINEN.

 # Purse

Size:

12 × 13cm (4¾ × 5in)

Materials:

15 × 18cm (6 × 7in) piece of 28-count (11 threads/cm) pink linen, DMC ref. 225
• 45 × 20cm (17¾ × 7¾in) piece of Liberty Tana Lawn (Ianthe) • DMC Special
Mouliné stranded cotton: 1 skein of each colour listed in the chart key • 15cm
(6in) length of 1cm (⅜in) wide silver ribbon • 15cm (6in) length of 1cm (⅜in)
wide lilac ribbon with orange polka dots • 25 × 10cm (9¾ × 4in) rectangle of stiff
interfacing • stainless-steel purse clasp, 8cm (3¼in) long • strong glue for textiles
and metals • sewing thread to match the fabric • sewing kit • fabric marker pen.
Refer to the chart on page 75 and the pattern on page 90.

EMBROIDERY

Mark out the position of the motif on the linen, centred 6cm
(2¼in) above the lower edge. Stitch the embroidery, working
each stitch over two linen threads and using two strands of
Special Mouliné thread for the cross stitch and backstitch (see
the chart).

SEWING

1 Making sure that the print on the Liberty fabric is the right
way up, cut three rectangles 14cm wide and 16cm high
(5½ × 6¼in) and one rectangle 14cm wide and 6cm high
(5½ × 2¼in).

2 Transfer the purse pattern to the wrong side of the
embroidered linen, aligning the broken line with the bottom
of the motif.

3 On the small rectangle of fabric, fold the upper edge over to
the wrong side by 1cm (⅜in) and press it. Attach this rectangle
beneath the embroidered motif using slip stitch. Attach the
silver ribbon just on top of the fabric and then attach the
polka-dot ribbon so that it overlaps the silver ribbon.

4 Pin the assembly to one of the large fabric rectangles with
right sides facing. Stitch on the outline of the linen,
following the shape of the purse pattern and leaving a gap
4cm (1½in) long in the centre of the upper edge. Trim the
seam allowances to 5mm (¼in) from the stitching. Turn right
side out.

5 Trace the purse pattern on to one of the remaining fabric
rectangles and then stitch the two rectangles together with
right sides facing in the same way. Trim the seam allowance
as in step 4 and turn the piece right side out.

6 Transfer the upper part of the pattern (above the broken line)
on to the stiff interfacing twice, then cut out. Slip one piece
of interfacing into each of the purse pieces. Fold the edges
of the openings inside and close up with slip stitch.

7 Paste the inside of the clasp with glue, insert the upper edge
of the two assemblies and leave to dry.

8 Join the front and back of the purse securely with
overcast stitch.

TIP

IF THE LINEN IS VERY FINE AND THE LIBERTY FABRIC SHOWS THROUGH, YOU
CAN LINE IT WITH A PLAIN, FINE, PALE FABRIC INSTEAD.

✻ Evening bag

Size:
28 × 13cm (11 × 5in)
Materials:
27 × 18cm (10¾ × 7in) piece of 28-count (11 threads/cm) dark beige linen, DMC ref. 842 • 90 × 30cm (35½ × 11¾in) piece of Liberty Tana Lawn (Peacock Feather) • 50 × 5cm (19¾ × 2in) strip of bright red fabric to make the berry decorations • DMC Special Mouliné stranded cotton: 1 skein of each colour listed in the chart key • 15cm (6in) length of ribbon with black and pink picot edges • 35 × 30cm (13¾ × 11¾in) rectangle of wadding (batting) • 25 × 15cm (9¾ × 6in) rectangle of stiff interfacing • a little synthetic wadding • 2cm (¾in) black press stud • sewing thread to match the fabric • repositionable fabric adhesive spray • sewing kit • quilting needle No. 7 • fabric marker pen • pair of compasses.
Refer to the chart on page 75 and the patterns on pages 94–95.

Embroidery

Mark the position of the motif on the linen, centred 4cm (1½in) above the lower long edge. Work each stitch over two linen threads, using two strands of Special Mouliné cotton for both the cross stitch and backstitch.

Flap

1 Transfer patterns C, D and E on to stiff interfacing and cut out.
2 Spray glue on one side of each piece. Place piece C on the wrong side of the embroidered linen, aligning the upper edge of piece C with the top of the motif. Arrange piece D above it, then piece E, with a space of 2–3mm (⅛in) between each one to allow for bending. Trim the linen 1.5cm (⅝in) from the interfacing. Turn the excess linen over the interfacing and fix in place using large slip stitches, taking care not to go through to the right side of the embroidery.
3 Place the assembly on the wrong side of the Liberty fabric and transfer the contour. Cut out the fabric, leaving a 1cm (⅜in) seam allowance all round. Fold the seam allowance to the back of the fabric and glue down. Glue the fabric to the back of the embroidered flap (you can lift the fabric carefully in order to adjust the fabric allowance level with the edges). Sew around the flap with slip stitch.

Main bag

1 Paying attention to the direction of the print, transfer pattern A once and pattern B twice to the wrong side of the Liberty fabric (transfer the reference marks of pattern A also). Cut out the three pieces adding a 1cm (⅜in) seam allowance all round.
2 Spray glue on to the wrong side of piece A and stick it to the wadding. Trim the wadding to match the fabric.
3 Quilt piece A by stitching around the feathers using Special Mouliné thread 816.
4 Make a box pleat by folding each mark X' over X in the centre, right sides together; the folds will meet in the middle. Secure the pleats by stitching just inside the fabric edge on each end.
5 Fold piece A in half, right sides together, so the ends of the pleat meet. Stitch the short sides 1cm (⅜in) from the edges, rounding the corners as on the pattern.
6 Place both lining pieces B right sides together and pin. Stitch all round, taking a 1cm (⅜in) seam allowance and leaving the straight top edge open. Turn right side out.
7 Pin the lining in the bag, right sides together. Stitch 1cm (⅜in) from the upper edge, leaving a small gap to turn the back through. Turn right side out. Turn in the edges of the gap and close up with slip stitch. Slip the lining (assembly B) inside the bag.
8 Pin the flap to the back of the bag and attach with discreet stitches into the layer of stiff interfacing.

Completing the bag

1 Sew the male part of the press stud in the centre of the underside of the flap and attach the female part to correspond on the bag front.
2 Cut out ten 3cm (1¼in) circles from the red fabric. Fold the edges to the wrong side by rolling between your index finger and thumb. Work a doubled gathering thread around the edge, fill with wadding and pull the thread to close up the fabric; fasten off. Sew the balls obtained on to the ribbon. Fold the ribbon in half and sew on to the body of the bag just above the press stud.

Tips

The fabric berries add the finishing touch to the bag. As an alternative you could use large beads or charms or even use a ready-made decoration.

Cut your patterns out of acetate sheets, available from craft and quilting suppliers, so that you can use them again and again. For this pattern, you will need 55 × 15cm (21¾ × 6in).

✳ Fancy earrings

Size:
3.5cm (1½in) diameter
Materials:
Two 'antique' metal earring fittings • two 10cm (4in) squares of 28-count (11 threads/cm) dark beige linen, DMC ref. 842 • 15 × 10cm (6 × 4in) piece of Liberty Tana Lawn (Millie) • DMC Special Mouliné stranded cotton: 1 skein of each colour listed in the chart key • 10 × 5cm (4 × 2in) piece of stiff interfacing • 5cm (2in) square of Bristol board • sewing thread to match the fabric • sewing kit • fabric marker pen • pair of compasses.
Refer to the chart on page 74.

EMBROIDERY

Embroider one motif in the centre of each linen square, working each cross stitch over one linen thread and using one strand of Special Mouliné cotton.

SEWING

1 Cut out two 3cm (1¼in) diameter circles from the stiff interfacing. Pin the embroidered linen squares on top, using the transparency of the fabric to help with positioning. Trim the linen 1.5cm (⅝in) from the interfacing. Using a double thread, working running stitch all round the embroidered linen. Pull the thread to gather the linen down over the interfacing and fasten off. Sew the linen overlap to the interfacing using large slip stitches, taking care not to go through to the right side of the embroidery.

2 Cut two 5cm (2in) fabric circles and one 3.5cm (1½in) circle of Bristol board. Work running stitch around the fabric circle, 5mm (¼in) from the edge, as before. Place the circle of Bristol board on the wrong side of the fabric and pull the thread to gather up the fabric around it; do not fasten off the thread yet. Press the fold then remove the Bristol board and fasten off the thread.

3 Pin the embroidered circles to the fabric circles, wrong sides together; the fabric circles will be slightly larger. Join the layers using slip stitch.

4 Stitch the earring fittings to the circles, positioning them as in the photographs.

❧ The little black dress revisited

Size:
Each embroidered motif is 4.5 × 14.5cm (1¾ × 5¾in)
Materials:
A dress or top with straps at least 4.5cm (1¾in) wide • two 10 × 55cm (4 × 21¾in)
pieces of 18-count (11 threads/cm) dark beige linen, DMC ref. 842 • 15 × 10cm
(6 × 4in) piece of Liberty Tana Lawn (Cranford) • DMC Special Mouliné stranded
cotton: 1 skein of each colour listed in the chart key • 10cm (4in) square of stiff
interfacing • sewing thread to match the linen and fabric • sewing kit • fabric
marker pen • pair of compasses.
Refer to the chart on page 73.

EMBROIDERY

Spread out one of the strips of linen with the short sides at the
top and bottom. Mark out the position of the first motif, centred
5cm (2in) from the lower edge. Embroider the design, working
each stitch over two linen threads and using two strands of
Special Mouliné cotton for both the cross stitch and the
backstitch. Repeat three times in all from bottom to top.
Embroider both pieces in the same way.

SEWING

1 Measure the length of the dress or top straps.
2 Fold each long side of each embroidered linen strip to the
   wrong side by 2.75cm (1in) to obtain a width of 4.5cm (2in),
   with the motifs in the centre. Fold the ends so the strip is
   the same length as the dress strap and then fold one of them
   into a point. Cut off the excess linen, 1cm (⅜in) from the
   folds all round.
3 Pin an embroidered strip to each strap with the pointed end
   at the front and attach with slip stitch.

TIP

IF YOU WISH TO MAKE YOUR OWN STRAPS FOR A DRESS OR TOP, CUT TWO
STRIPS FROM THE LIBERTY FABRIC 6.5CM (2½IN) WIDE BY THE REQUIRED
LENGTH PLUS 2CM (¾IN). PRESS 1CM (⅜IN) TO THE WRONG SIDE ALL
ROUND EACH STRIP AND PRESS. PIN THE STRIPS OF FABRIC BENEATH THE
STRIPS OF LINEN, WRONG SIDES FACING, THEN STITCH AROUND THE EDGES
WITH SLIP STITCH.

FINISHING TOUCHES

1 Cut out two 3cm (1¼in) circles from stiff interfacing and two 6cm (2¼in) circles from the Liberty fabric.

2 Using a double thread, work running stitch around each fabric circle, 5mm (¼in) from the edge. Place a circle of interfacing on the back of the fabric and pull the thread to gather the fabric over it; fasten off. Sew one of these two false buttons at the pointed end of each strap.

3 You can add further embellishment to the dress by adding a yoke. Use the dress or top as a pattern for its shape. Transfer the pattern on to the wrong side of the fabric and then cut out adding a 1cm (⅜in) seam allowance all around. Press the seam allowance to the wrong side then pin the yoke to the garment and sew in place around the edges using slip stitch.

TIPS

IF YOUR DRESS OR TOP HAS ITS OWN BUTTONS, COVER THEM WITH FABRIC TO MATCH THE STRAPS AS FOR THE FALSE BUTTONS (CUT OUT A CIRCLE OF FABRIC TWICE AS BIG AS THE BUTTON EACH TIME). ALTERNATIVELY MAKE FABRIC-COVERED BUTTONS TO FIT THE BUTTONHOLES USING A KIT.

USE MORE LIBERTY FABRIC TO TRIM POCKET EDGES OR EVEN THE HEM OF THE DRESS. JUST MEASURE THE EDGE TO BE TRIMMED AND CUT A PIECE TO FIT, ADDING 1CM (⅜IN) SEAM ALLOWANCES ALL ROUND. PRESS THE SEAM ALLOWANCES TO THE BACK OF THE FABRIC AND SLIP STITCH THE TRIMMING IN PLACE.

2. In the home

Photo frames

Round cushion

Elegant placemat

Tea pouch

Charming needle case

Decorative stickers

Colourful pot holders

Box of secrets

❋ Photo frames

Size:
13 × 18cm (5 × 7in)
For the embroidery:
20 × 25cm (7¾ × 9¾in) piece of 28-count (11 threads/cm) dark beige linen, DMC ref. 842 • DMC Special Mouliné stranded cotton: 1 skein of each colour listed in the chart key.
Materials for each of the three frames:
13 × 18cm (5 × 7in) frame • Liberty Tana Lawn (Burnham): 40 × 5cm (15¾ × 2in) strip for the corner frame; 20 × 25cm (7¾ × 9¾in) rectangle for the unembroidered frame • Liberty Tana Lawn (Glenjade): 45 × 25cm (17¾ × 9¾in) rectangle for the corner frame; 95 × 25cm (37½ × 9¾in) for the ruched frame and the unembroidered frame • 20cm (7¾in) square of stiff interfacing • repositionable fabric adhesive spray • double-sided adhesive tape • sewing thread to match the fabrics • sewing kit • fabric marker penture.
Refer to the charts on pages 76–77 and the pattern on page 90.

EMBROIDERY

Centre the motif on the linen using the red reference marks on the charts. Work each stitch over two linen threads, using two strands of Special Mouliné cotton for the cross stitch and one strand for the backstitch.

FRAME APERTURE

1 Cut a 13 × 18cm (5 × 7in) rectangle of stiff interfacing. Trace an oval in the centre using the pattern, then cut it out with a pair of small pointed scissors.
2 Centre the embroidered linen carefully on the interfacing and pin in place – for the unembroidered frame use the 20 × 25cm (7¾ × 9¾in) rectangle of Liberty fabric instead. Trim away the fabric 1.5cm (⅝in) inside the oval – this margin is for a turning. Snip into the turning allowance at regular intervals up to the interfacing, then turn the fabric over the interfacing around the oval aperture and around the outer edges of the interfacing. Sew the linen allowance to the interfacing using large slip stitches, taking care not to go through to the right side.

CORNER FRAME DECORATIONS

1 Cut four 9 × 3cm (3½ × 1¼in) strips of Burnham fabric and fold each one in half lengthways, wrong sides together, to obtain a 9 × 1.5cm (3½ × ⅝in) strip. Press the strips.

2 Cut two 10cm (4in) squares from the Glenjade fabric and then cut them diagonally to obtain four triangles. Fold each diagonal edge to the wrong side by 1cm (⅜in) and press the fold.

3 Place one fabric strip under the diagonal of each triangle, allowing it to overhang by 8mm (⅜in). Pin the triangles to the four corners of the embroidered linen, making them overhang by 5mm (¼in) on the outside. Turn down the excess fabric at the back of the interfacing and sew with slip stitch.

RUCHED FRAME DECORATIONS

1 Cut a 70 × 3cm (27½ × 1¼in) strip from the Glenjade fabric. Fold each side over 7mm (¼in) to the wrong side and press. With a long length of thread, stitch along the strip in a wavy line (sinusoidal). Pull up the thread until the strip fits around the oval aperture with enough left over for an overlap to hide the raw edges; fasten off.

2 Pin the ruched strip around the oval aperture on the right side. Fold its ends wrong sides together and then sew using discreet stitches.

DECORATIONS FOR THE UNEMBROIDERED FRAME

Make a ruched strip as explained for the previous frame. Attach it around the oval aperture on the wrong side so that half of it shows on the right side.

ASSEMBLY

Note: use the Glenjade fabric for the embroidered frames and the Burnham fabric for the unembroidered one.

1 From interfacing cut two 1.5 × 18cm (⅝ × 7in) strips and two 1.5 × 13cm (⅝ × 5in) strips. From fabric cut two 5 × 20cm (2 × 7¾in) strips and two 5 × 15cm (2 × 6in) strips. Spray glue on to the wrong side of the strips of fabric and place the corresponding strips of interfacing on top, leaving a margin of 1cm (⅜in) on three sides and 2.5cm (1in) along the remaining long edge. Press the three 1cm (⅜in) margins over the interfacing. Fold the fourth side over by 1cm (⅜in) then glue the remaining fabric over the interfacing – the two long edges should meet.

2 Working with overcast stitch, sew the strips to the back of the embroidered linen, one along each edge of the frame, then join at the four corners. This fabric frame will hold the picture frame inside.

3 Stick a piece of double-sided adhesive tape to the four corners, under the fabric frame, then slip the picture frame in place.

TIP

IF YOU CANNOT FIND A PLAIN PICTURE FRAME TO FIT INSIDE YOUR DECORATIVE FRAME, SIMPLY CUT A 13 × 18CM (5 × 7IN) RECTANGLE OF HARDBOARD AND ATTACH PICTURE FIXINGS TO THE BACK TO HANG IT BY. INSTEAD OF GLASS, CUT A PIECE OF ACETATE TO PROTECT YOUR CHOSEN PICTURE OR PHOTOGRAPH.

✿ Round cushion

Size:
40cm (15¾in) diameter
Materials:
30 × 30cm (11¾ × 11¾in) piece of 28-count (11 threads/cm) dark beige linen, DMC ref. 842 • 135 × 25cm (53¼ × 9¾in) piece of Liberty City Poplin (Pani Gabriela) or other cotton fabric of your choice (fabric A) • 135 × 25cm (53¼ × 9¾in) piece of Liberty fabric (Hurrel) or other cotton of your choice (fabric B) • DMC Special Mouliné stranded cotton: 1 skein of each colour listed in the chart key • 25cm (9¾in) square of stiff interfacing • synthetic wadding • strong sewing thread to match the fabrics • sewing set (a sewing machine is recommended) • fabric marker pen • pair of compasses.
Refer to the chart on page 78 and the joining diagram on page 91.

EMBROIDERY
Embroider the motif in the centre of the linen, working each stitch over two linen threads and using two strands of Special Mouliné cotton.

PATCHWORK
1 From each of the two fabrics cut the following: one 22 × 23cm (8¾ × 9in) rectangle, one 27 × 23cm (10¾ × 9in) rectangle and two 42 × 23cm (16½ × 9in) rectangles.
2 Arrange the rectangles in two strips as shown in the diagram on page 91. Join the short sides by stitching 1cm (⅜in) from the edges, with right sides facing, to obtain two strips measuring 127 × 23cm (50 × 9in). Lay one strip over the other with right sides facing. Stitch one of the long sides, taking a 1cm (⅜in) seam allowance, to obtain a patchwork measuring 127 × 44cm (50 × 17¼in). Press the seam open. Overlay the two short sides, right sides together, and stitch 1cm (⅜in) from the edge. Turn the tube obtained right side out.

ASSEMBLY
1 With a long double length of strong thread, work running stitch 5mm (¼in) from one of the edges of the tube, stitching all around the edge (the density of the linen prevents a turn in before this). Pull the thread to gather the fabric as much as possible and then fasten off with a few little backstitches overlaid. Fold the piece along the long central seam in the patchwork, right sides out, and stuff with the wadding, distributing it particularly around what will be the outer edge (the long centre seam in the patchwork) in order to form a circle. Close up the other edge by gathering as before.

2 With a long length of strong thread doubled over, make large stitches right through the cushion to flatten out a circle with a diameter of 20cm (7¾in) in the centre (where the embroidery will go).
3 Trace a circle with a diameter of 21cm (8¼in) on the stiff interfacing, then cut out.
4 Place the embroidered linen on the interfacing, being careful to centre the motif, then pin through both layers. Trim the linen 1.5cm (⅝in) outside the interfacing. Use a double thread to work running stitch in this margin and pull up to gather the linen down over the interfacing; fasten off. Sew the linen allowance to the interfacing with large slip stitches, taking care not to go through to the right side of the embroidery.
5 Pin the embroidered linen to the centre of the cushion, then stitch it in place around the edge with slip stitch.

❋ Elegant placemat

Size:
46 × 33cm (18 × 13in)
Materials:
20 × 40cm (7¾ × 15¾in) piece of 28-count (11 threads/cm) dark beige linen, DMC
ref. 842 • 32 × 33cm (12½ × 13in) piece of grey linen • 49 × 36cm (19¼ × 14¼in)
piece of Liberty Tana Lawn (Glenjade) • DMC Special Mouliné stranded cotton: 1
skein of each shade listed in the chart key • sewing thread to match the fabric
• sewing kit (a sewing machine is recommended) • fabric marker pen.
Refer to the chart on page 79.

EMBROIDERY

Mark out the position of the motif on the dark beige linen,
centred 5cm (2in) above the lower edge. Work each stitch
over two linen threads using two strands of Special Mouliné
cotton for the cross stitch and one strand for the backstitch and
French knots.

SEWING

1 Trace a 16 × 33cm (6¼ × 13in) rectangle on the
   embroidered linen: the motif must be centred 2.5cm (1in)
   above the lower edge. Cut the rectangle.
2 Place the grey linen on the embroidered linen with right
   sides facing and matching the left edge of the embroidered
   piece. Stitch the seam 1cm (⅜in) from the edge. Press the
   seam carefully on the right side.
3 Fold the four sides of the Liberty fabric over by 5mm (¼in)
   and press to the back. Centre the embroidered linen on the
   back of the fabric and pin across all the layers. Turn down
   the fabric over the linen along all the edges, pin and then
   sew neatly in place using slip stitch.

❦ Tea pouch

Size:
7cm (2¾in) wide, 4cm (1½in) deep and 21cm (8¼in) high
Materials:
28-count (11 threads/cm) pink linen, DMC ref. 225: an 18 × 30cm (7 × 11¾in) rectangle for the front and base and a 9 × 24.5cm (3½ × 9¾in) rectangle for the back • two 6 × 23cm (2¼in × 9in) rectangles of Liberty Tana Lawn (Sarah's Secret Garden) for the sides • DMC Special Mouliné stranded cotton: 1 skein of each colour listed in the chart key • traditional wooden clothes peg • sewing thread to match the fabric • sewing kit • fabric marker pen.

Refer to the chart on page 85 and the folding diagram on page 91.

EMBROIDERY

Position the motif on the 18 × 30cm (7 × 11¾in) linen rectangle by placing the red reference mark in the chart 6cm (2¼in) from the right side and lower edge. Work each stitch over two threads of linen, using two strands of Special Mouliné cotton for the cross stitch and one strand for the backstitch and French knots.

FOLDING

1   Make the folds that form the tea pouch with wrong sides together. First fold over the long right edge 4mm (⅛in) from the embroidery, then fold the long left edge 7cm (2¾in) to the left of the first fold; fold the lower edge 4mm (⅛in) beneath the embroidery, then 4cm (1½in) lower. Continue folding, following the diagram on page 91, and then trim off the excess linen along the sides and lower edge.

2   Form the front, sides and base of the pouch by folding the surplus linen of the bottom corners diagonally, then secure the shape using overcast stitch.

SEWING

1   The remaining linen rectangle forms the back of the pouch. Fold the two long sides and lower edge over to the wrong side by 1cm (⅜in); press. Join this rectangle to the long sides and bottom of the embroidered linen.

2   Lay out both fabric rectangles and press 1cm (⅜in) to the wrong side all round. Slip stitch the fabric rectangles to the sides of the sachet.

3   Fold the upper edge of the two pieces of linen inside to obtain a pouch 21cm (8¼in) high. Close the pouch using the clothes peg.

✿ Charming needle case

Size when closed:
8.5cm (3¼in) square
Materials:
40 × 15cm (15¾ × 6in) rectangle of 28-count (11 threads/cm) off-white linen, DMC ref. 712 • Liberty Tana Lawn (Williams): 36 × 12cm (14¼ × 4¾in) rectangle for the inside; ten 3cm (1¼in) squares for the flowers; four 15 × 2cm (6 × ¾in) rectangles for the ties • DMC Special Mouliné stranded cotton: 1 skein of each colour listed in the chart key • four 7.5 × 8cm (3 × 3¼in) pieces of stiff interfacing • fabric adhesive spray • sewing thread to match the fabric • sewing kit • fabric marker pen.
Refer to the chart on pages 80–81.

EMBROIDERY

Embroider the motif in the centre of the linen, working each stitch over two linen threads. Use two strands of Special Mouliné cotton for the cross stitch and one strand for the backstitch and French knots.

SEWING

1 Fold the edges of the embroidered linen to the wrong side to produce a 32 × 8.5cm (12½ × 3¼in) rectangle with the motif in the centre. Trim the excess linen 1cm (⅜in) from the folds.

2 Spray the glue on to one side of each rectangle of stiff interfacing, then fix these on to the wrong side of the embroidered linen: place each one 2.5mm (⅛in) from the edges and leave a space of 5mm (¼in) between them. On the wrong side of the 36 × 12cm (14¼ × 4¾in) fabric rectangle,

trace a rectangle measuring 32.75 × 8.75cm (13 × 3½in) in the centre. Fold each edge to the wrong side along the marked lines and then press. Pin the embroidered linen centrally to the fabric, with wrong sides together, and join around the edges using slip stitch.

3 Fold each of the ten squares diagonally, wrong sides together. Bring the sides towards the point of the middle by folding, then secure with a few small overlaid backstitches. These are the flowers.

4 On each of the four strips of fabric, fold the four sides over to the back by 5mm (¼in) then fold the strips in half lengthways and press. Close up with overcast stitch, inserting the flowers here and there. Fold the ties in two asymmetrically, then sew them on to the needle holder: place one centred at each end of the fabric and place the two others on the linen fold lines, as shown in the photographs.

❧ Decorative stickers

Size:
10.5cm (4¼in) in diameter
Materials for each embroidered sticker:
20 × 20cm (7¾ × 7¾in) piece of 28-count (11 threads/cm) ivory linen, DMC ref. 3865 • DMC Special Mouliné stranded cotton: 1 skein of each colour listed in the key • 15cm (6in) square of stiff interfacing • double-sided adhesive tape • sewing thread • sewing kit • fabric marker pen • pair of compasses.
Materials for each unembroidered sticker:
Use the same materials as for the embroidered stickers but without the embroidery cotton and replacing the linen with a 15cm (6in) square of Liberty Tana Lawn (Haxby).
Refer to the charts on pages 84–85.

EMBROIDERY

Embroider your chosen motif in the centre of the linen, working each stitch over two linen threads. Use two strands of Special Mouliné cotton for the cross stitch and one strand for the backstitch.

SEWING

1 Trace a 10.5cm (4¼in) diameter circle on the stiff interfacing and cut out.

2 Centre the embroidered linen on the interfacing and then pin through both layers. Trim the excess linen 1.5cm (⅝in) from the interfacing.

3 Using a double thread, work running stitch in the margin around the edge of the fabric. Pull the thread to gather the linen down over the interfacing and then fasten off. Sew the linen overlap to the interfacing with large slip stitches, taking care not to go through to the right side of the embroidery.

4 Fix your stickers to the required spots with double-sided adhesive tape.

TIP
THESE DESIGNS COULD ALSO BE USED TO MAKE PRETTY PATCHES TO SEW ON POCKETS OR BAGS, AND THEY WOULD MAKE CHARMING FRAMED PICTURES.

❊ Colourful pot holders

Size:

9cm (3½in) diameter and 11cm (4¼in) high

Materials for each embroidered pot holder:

50 × 30cm (19¾ × 11¾in) piece of 28-count (11 threads/cm) ivory linen, DMC ref. 3865 • 40 × 25cm (15¾ × 9¾in) rectangle of Liberty Tana Lawn (Droxford) • DMC Special Mouliné stranded cotton: 1 skein of each colour listed in the chart key • 40 × 25cm (15¾ × 9¾in) rectangle of stiff interfacing • repositionable fabric adhesive spray • sewing thread to match the fabric • sewing kit • fabric marker pen.

Materials for each unembroidered pot holder:

Use the same materials as for the embroidered pot holders but without the embroidery cotton and replacing the linen with a 45 × 25cm (17¾ × 9¾in) rectangle of Liberty fabric.

Refer to the charts on pages 80–83 and the pattern on page 92.

EMBROIDERY

Embroider the motif in the centre of the linen, working each stitch over two linen threads. Use two strands of Special Mouliné cotton for the cross stitch and one strand for the backstitch and French knots.

SEWING

1 Spray the glue on to the wrong side of the fabric and fix the stiff interfacing on top. Transfer the pattern on to the interfacing and then cut out around the shape.

2 Position the embroidered linen on the other side of the interfacing, ensuring that the motifs are in the correct position and then pin through all the layers. Trim off the linen 1.5cm (⅝in) from the interfaced fabric. Fold 5mm (¼in) to the wrong side, iron and then turn the allowance over the interfaced fabric. Pin the folded linen through all layers and then attach to the fabric with slip stitch.

3 Overlay the two short sides, linen against linen, and join with overcast stitch. Turn the pot holder right side out.

TIP

CUT YOUR PATTERN OUT OF ACETATE, AVAILABLE FROM CRAFT AND QUILTING SUPPLIERS, SO THAT YOU CAN USE IT AGAIN AND AGAIN. FOR THIS PATTERN, YOU WILL NEED 20 × 15CM (7¾ × 6IN).

❋ Box of secrets

Size:
8cm (3¼in) wide, 13cm (5in) long and 3cm (1¼in) high
Materials:
15 × 20cm (6 × 7¾in) piece of 28-count (11 threads/cm) ivory linen, DMC ref. 3865 • 60 × 20cm (23½ × 7¾in) piece of Liberty Tana Lawn (Capel) • 60cm (23½in) length of bright orange ribbon • DMC Special Mouliné stranded cotton: 1 skein of each colour listed in the chart key • 30 × 15cm (11¾ × 6in) rectangle of stiff interfacing • repositionable fabric adhesive spray • sewing thread to match the fabric • sewing kit • fabric marker pen.
Refer to the chart on page 87.

EMBROIDERY

Embroider the motif in the centre of the linen, working each stitch over two linen threads. Use two strands of Special Mouliné cotton for the cross stitch and one strand for the backstitch.

SEWING

1 From the fabric cut one 40 × 15cm (15¾ × 6in) rectangle and two 10 × 8cm (4 × 3¼in) rectangles.
2 From stiff interfacing cut out one 8 × 13cm (3¼ × 5in) rectangle, two 3 × 13cm (1¼ × 5in) strips, two 3.75 × 13cm (1½ × 5in) strips and two 8 × 3cm (3¼ × 1¼in) strips.
3 Spray glue on to the wrong side of the large rectangle of fabric. Centre the rectangle of interfacing on top and on each side place one 3 × 13cm (1¼ × 5in) strip and then one 3.75 × 13cm (1½ × 5in) strip, leaving a very small gap between each one to allow the fabric to bend. Apply glue to the surplus fabric and turn first the long sides over the interfacing and then the short sides. Secure the turnings using slip stitch.
4 Spray glue on to the wrong side of the two remaining rectangles of fabric. Place the remaining strips of interfacing on top, leaving a margin of 1cm (⅜in) on three sides. Turn down these three sides over the interfacing. Fold the fourth side over 1cm (⅜in) then fold the whole strip in half lengthways (along the edge of the interfacing) and glue down.
5 Working in overcast stitch, join one strip to the top and one to the bottom of the central panel of the main section. Fold up the sides in order to form the box and stitch in place.
6 Fold the four edges of the embroidered linen to the wrong side in order to obtain an 8 × 13cm (3¼ × 5in) rectangle.

Trim off the surplus linen 1cm (⅜in) from the folds. Place the linen in the bottom of the box. Secure the box flaps by tying the ribbon around the box.

TIP
THIS BOX WOULD BE IDEAL FOR HOLDING A DIARY, SMALL SKETCHBOOK OR NOTEBOOK, PERHAPS CONTAINING POEMS OR DESIGNS. IF YOU ALREADY HAVE A JOURNAL OR NOTEBOOK THAT YOU WOULD LIKE TO STORE, YOU CAN EASILY ADAPT THE INSTRUCTIONS ABOVE TO MAKE A SECRETS BOX TO FIT.

3. For baby

Little slippers

Handy little bag

Soft bricks

Bottle holder

Garland

Rattle

Book cover

Soft quilt

❧ Little slippers

Size:
Birth/first few months
Materials:
Two 10 × 15cm (4 × 6in) pieces of 28-count (11 threads/cm) ivory linen, DMC ref. 3865
• 25 × 15cm (9¾ × 6in) piece of Liberty Tana Lawn (Miles Evans, pink) • 50 × 5cm (19¾ × 2in)
strip of bright orange cotton fabric for the ties (see the tip, below) • 15cm (6in) square of
lightweight orange felt to line the soles • DMC Special Mouliné stranded cotton: 1 skein of
each colour listed in the chart key • 15cm (6in) square of stiff interfacing • 20 × 15cm (7¾ × 6in)
rectangle of fusible webbing (Bondaweb) • repositionable fabric adhesive spray • sewing
thread to match the fabric • sewing kit • fabric marker pen.
Refer to the chart on page 88 and the patterns on page 94.

EMBROIDERY

Embroider the motif in the centre of each of the linen rectangles,
working each stitch over two linen threads. Use two strands of
Special Mouliné cotton for both the cross stitch and backstitch.

SOLES

1 Transfer the sole pattern (A) to the stiff interfacing twice,
   flipping it for the second sole to make a pair. Cut out the soles.
2 Place one embroidered linen rectangle over each sole and
   centre the motifs, using the transparency of the material to help
   you. Trim the linen 1cm (⅜in) from the interfacing. Fold the
   fabric allowance over the interfacing and attach it with large
   slip stitches, taking care not to go through to the right side.
3 Spray glue on to one side of the felt. Place the soles on top,
   interfacing side down, and trim the felt level with the linen.

UPPERS

1 Transfer the pattern for the uppers (B) to fusible webbing
   twice. Cut out the uppers then cut along the vertical slit line.
2 Cut out four 6 × 12cm (2¼ × 4¾in) rectangles of fabric. On
   each rectangle, press one of the long edges over to the wrong
   side by 1cm (⅜in). Lay out two of these rectangles wrong
   sides up, with the turned in edges touching. Fuse one
   fusible-webbing upper on top, aligning the slit on the upper
   so that it lies between the turn-ins, and leaving a fabric
   allowance all round. Slip stitch the turn-ins together
   from X to the slit. Fold the fabric over the webbing around
   the edges and press with your fingers. Trim the fabric edges,
   where necessary, leaving a 1cm (⅜in) fabric allowance.
   Prepare the other upper in the same way using the two
   remaining rectangles of fabric.
3 Transfer the pattern for the uppers (B) to the wrong side of
   the Liberty fabric twice. Cut out, leaving a 1cm (⅜in) turning
   allowance all around, then cut the slit, extending it by
   5mm (¼in).

4 Fold a small hem to the wrong side on each edge of the slit,
   letting it taper at the point of the slit. Press the 1cm (⅜in)
   turning allowance to the wrong side around the edges. Place
   these pieces under the backed uppers, with wrong sides
   facing, and stitch around the edges with slip stitch.

ASSEMBLY

1 Working in overcast stitch, close up the back of the uppers
   (the straight top edge of the pattern) then sew an upper to
   each sole.
2 Cut two 25 × 3cm (9¾ × 1¼in) strips from the orange fabric.
   Tie each one into a bow and sew it to the front of a slipper
   using discreet stitches.

TIPS
CUT YOUR PATTERN OUT OF ACETATE, AVAILABLE FROM CRAFT AND QUILTING
SUPPLIERS, SO THAT YOU CAN USE IT AGAIN AND AGAIN. FOR THIS PATTERN,
YOU WILL NEED ABOUT 15CM (6IN) SQUARE.
USE TWO LENGTHS OF ORANGE RIBBON, EACH 25CM (10IN) LONG, INSTEAD
OF CUTTING THE BOWS FROM FABRIC. USE METALLIC OR VELVET RIBBON FOR
AN EXTRA TOUCH OF LUXURY. IF YOU USE A DIFFERENT COLOUR FOR THE
BOWS, CHANGE THE COLOUR OF THE FELT INNER SOLES AS WELL.

✳ Handy little bag

Size:
14.5cm × 16cm (5¾ × 6¼in)

Materials:
20 × 10cm (7¾ × 4in) piece of 28-count (11 threads/cm) dark beige linen, DMC ref. 842 • 16.5 × 36cm (6½ × 14¼in) piece of Liberty Tana Lawn (Pepper) • 1m (39¼in) fluorescent yellow ribbon, 3mm (⅛in) wide • DMC Special Mouliné stranded cotton: 1 skein of each colour listed in the chart key • DMC Light Effect Mouliné cotton: 1 skein of E 980 (to attach the button only) • 1cm (⅜in) green button • sewing thread to match the fabric • sewing kit • safety pin • fabric marker pen. Refer to the chart on page 86.

EMBROIDERY

Embroider the motif in the centre of each of the linen rectangles, working each stitch over two linen threads. Use two strands of Special Mouliné cotton for both the cross stitch and backstitch.

SEWING

1 Fold all four edges of the embroidered linen to the wrong side to obtain a rectangle measuring 14.5 × 6cm (5¾ × 2½in), with the motif in the centre. Trim off the excess fabric 1cm (⅜in) from the folds.

2 Cut a 3cm (1¼in) length of ribbon and fold it in half. Sew its ends to the centre of the upper edge of the embroidered linen, on the wrong side, to make a button loop. Pin the linen to the right side of the fabric so it is centred 12cm (4¾in) from the upper edge. Attach it with slip stitch. Sew the button on to the fabric with the Light Effect Mouliné cotton E 980, so it sits inside the button loop.

3 Fold the fabric in half with right sides facing, level with the linen, and stitch the sides 1cm (⅜in) from the edges, stopping 2cm (¾in) from the upper edge. Fold the edges of the slits over to the wrong side by 1cm (⅜in).

4 Fold the upper edges over by 1cm (⅜in) then over again to the wrong side to make a casing for the ribbon tie; hem. Turn the bag right side out.

5 Cut the remaining ribbon into two equal lengths. Using the safety pin, thread one ribbon through the hems, starting and finishing at the same side of the bag; tie the ends together in a knot. Repeat with the other ribbon, starting and finishing at the other side of the bag.

TIP

WE ALL KNOW THAT BABY ITEMS CAN GET MESSY AT TIMES, SO SLIP A SMALL, STRONG PLASTIC BAG INSIDE THE EMBROIDERED BAG TO USE AS A DISPOSABLE LINER.

✳ Soft bricks

Size:
10 × 10 × 10cm (4 × 4 × 4in)
Materials for two bricks:
Four 15cm (6in) squares of 28-count (11 threads/cm) white linen, DMC ref. White
• two 15cm (6in) squares of baby pink linen • four 15cm (6in) squares of Liberty
Tana Lawn, (Kinnear) • two 15cm (6in) squares of baby blue fabric • DMC Special
Mouliné stranded cotton: 1 skein of each colour listed in the chart key • twelve
10cm (4in) squares of stiff interfacing • two 6cm (2¼in) lengths of 8mm (¼in)
wide silver ribbon to make hanging loops • 10cm (4in) square of Bristol board
• repositionable fabric adhesive spray • sewing thread to match the fabric
• sewing kit • fabric marker pen.
Refer to the charts on page 86.

EMBROIDERY

Position a motif on each of the white linen squares, using the red arrows in the chart to centre it. Embroider the design, working each stitch over two linen threads and using two strands of Special Mouliné cotton for both the cross stitch and backstitch.

SEWING

1 Centre the square of Bristol board on the wrong side of one of the embroidered squares. Fold the excess linen over the Bristol board and mark the folds clearly. Remove the Bristol board then cut off the excess linen 2cm (¾in) from the folds. Repeat with each embroidered square.

2 Spray glue on to one side of each square of stiff interfacing. Fix the linen and fabric squares on to them, centring them correctly. Glue the excess linen or fabric down over the back of the interfacing and sew in place using large slip stitches and taking care not to go through to the right side.

3 Make each brick by joining six squares with overcast stitch – distribute the fabrics and linens by taking inspiration from the photographs. On the last edge, slip the ends of a ribbon folded in half between the two squares and trap in the stitching to make a hanging loop.

TIPS
QUILTING SUPPLIERS USUALLY SELL FABRICS IN SMALL AMOUNTS, AND SINCE YOU ONLY NEED LITTLE PIECES FOR THIS PROJECT, THIS COULD BE A GOOD PLACE TO FIND THE FABRICS YOU NEED.
THESE SOFT BRICKS MAKE WONDERFUL HANGING DECORATIONS FOR A BABY'S ROOM. YOU COULD EASILY MAKE SOME SMALLER VERSIONS TO CREATE A PRETTY MOBILE BY WORKING ON A FINER LINEN FABRIC OR BY STITCHING ONLY ONE SECTION OF EACH DESIGN.

❀ Bottle holder

Size:
9 × 22cm (3½ × 8¾in)
Materials:
10 × 30cm (4 × 11¾in) strip of 28-count (11 threads/cm) ivory linen, DMC ref.
3865 • two 4 × 24cm (1½ × 9½in) strips of Liberty Tana Lawn (Toria, pink) • 50cm
(19¾in) square of Liberty Tana Lawn (Toria, coral) • DMC Special Mouliné
stranded cotton: 1 skein of each colour listed in the chart key • 60 × 10cm
(23½ × 4in) strip of stiff interfacing • Fine cord: one 20cm (7¾in) length and one
30cm (11¾in) length • repositionable fabric adhesive spray • sewing thread to
match the fabric • sewing kit • fabric marker pen • pair of compasses.
Refer to the chart on page 87.

EMBROIDERY

Embroider the motif in the centre of the linen, working each
stitch over two linen threads. Use two strands of Special Mouliné
cotton for the cross stitch and one strand for the backstitch.

SEWING

1 Cut out a 5 × 22cm (2 × 8¾in) rectangle of stiff interfacing.
   Centre it on the wrong side of the embroidered linen and pin
   in place. Turn the excess linen over the interfacing, then
   trim it 1cm (⅜in) from the folds.

2 On each of the two pink strips of fabric fold the short edges
   to the wrong side by 1cm (⅜in) and then fold the strip in half
   lengthways. Place one of these strips on each side of the
   embroidery so that the folded edge extends 1cm (⅜in) to the
   side of the embroidery (see the photographs).

3 Cut out one 28.25 × 22cm (11 × 8¾in) rectangle of
   interfacing and one 30.25 × 46cm (12 × 18in) rectangle of
   coral fabric. Lay out the fabric, right side down, with the
   long edges at the sides, spray with adhesive and then stick
   the interfacing on it, 1cm (⅜in) from the lower edge and
   sides. Fold the upper and lower edges over by 1cm (⅜in).
   The fabric is now 44cm (17¼in) long with the interfacing
   finishing at the halfway point. Fold the side edges over by
   1cm (⅜in) and then apply more glue and fold the fabric in
   half along the edge of the interfacing. Sew the edges with
   large slip stitches, taking care not to go through to the right
   side. Join the two short ends, edge to edge, using overcast
   stitch. Pin on the embroidered linen, centring it over the
   stitching, and then attach using slip stitch.

4 Cut out one 9cm (3½in) diameter circle of interfacing and
   one 18cm (7in) diameter circle of coral fabric. With a long
   length of double thread, work running stitch 5mm (¼in) from
   the edge of the fabric (the density of the fabric prevents
   making a turn-in before this). Pin the circle of interfacing in
   the centre of the fabric circle, on the wrong side, and pull
   the thread to gather the fabric over the top. Fasten off.
   Working in overcast stitch, join the circle to the base of the
   interfaced tube.

5 From coral fabric cut one 1.5 × 21cm (⅝ × 8¼in) strip and
   one 1.5 × 31cm (⅝ × 12¼in) strip. On each one, fold the
   four sides over to the wrong side by 5mm (¼in) and press.
   Fold each strip around the corresponding length of cord,
   close up the long edges with slip stitch and then make a
   knot at each end. Sew the longest cord to the upper edge of
   the holder to make a handle, and knot the other on top of the
   handle asymmetrically.

 Garland

Size:
2m (78¾in) long; each pennant measures 5cm (2in) square

Materials:
Fifteen 17cm (6¾in) squares of 28-count (11 threads/cm) ivory linen, DMC ref. 3865 • eight 17cm (6¾in) squares of Liberty Tana Lawn (Tuesday Trees) • DMC Special Mouliné stranded cotton: 1 skein of each colour listed in the chart key • 2m (78¾in) of 4mm (⅛in) wide fluorescent yellow ribbon • 5cm (2in) square of Bristol board • sewing thread to match the linen and fabric • sewing kit.

Refer to the charts on page 82.

EMBROIDERY

Embroider a motif in the centre of each linen square, using the red arrows to help you. Repeat the motifs as required. Work each stitch over two linen threads, using two strands of Special Mouliné cotton.

FOLDING

Centre the Bristol board square on the wrong side of one of the embroidered squares, using the transparency of the material to help you. Turn the right and left sides over the Bristol board, crease well and then trim the linen 1cm (⅜in) from the folds. Repeat with the upper edge. Fold the lower edge up so that it covers the whole of the back and crease a fold along the top of the board; trim 1cm (⅜in) above the fold. In this way you create a backing. Remove the Bristol board and fold in all the seam allowances. Repeat with each square of embroidered linen.

JOINING

1 Fold the eight squares of Liberty fabric in the same way as the linen.
2 Arrange all the squares in a line, distributing the embroidered motifs and the fabric evenly. Slip the ribbon under the top fold of the first square, making it overhang by 20.5cm (8in) on one side (in order to hang up the garland). Close up the two edges of linen with slip stitch, stitching the ribbon also. Fix the remaining squares on to the ribbon, working in the same way and leaving a space of 2cm (¾in) between each one.

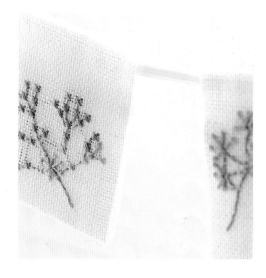

✳ Rattle

Size:
7cm (2¾in) diameter, 14cm (5½in) long
Materials:
4 × 25cm (1½ × 9¾in) strip of 28-count (11 threads/cm) dark beige linen, DMC ref. 842
• Liberty Tana Lawn (Winter Dreams of Spring): two 14cm (5½in) diameter circles for the main part (see the Tip below); four 4cm (1½in) circles for the little balls and two 2 × 13cm (¾ × 5in) strips for the ball ties • two 4cm (1½in) diameter circles of bright orange fabric • DMC Special Mouliné stranded cotton: 1 skein of each colour listed in the chart key • two 7cm (2¾in) diameter circles of stiff interfacing • synthetic wadding • 7cm (2¾in) long handle in turned wood • ten little bells • sewing thread to match the fabric • sewing kit • fabric marker pen • pair of compasses.
Refer to the charts on page 83.

EMBROIDERY
Embroider the motif in the centre of the linen, working each stitch over one linen thread and using one strand of Special Mouliné cotton.

SEWING
1 Fold the four sides of the embroidered linen to the wrong side to obtain a strip measuring 2 × 22cm (¾ × 8¾in) with the motif in the centre. Cut off any excess linen 1cm (⅜in) from the folds.
2 Work running stitch around each of the large circles of fabric, 5mm (¼in) from the edge, using a long length of double thread (the density of the fabric prevents a turn in from being made before this). Pin a circle of interfacing in the centre, on the wrong side, and pull the thread to gather the fabric in over it; fasten off.
3 Working with small, tight overcast stitches, join the embroidered linen around the interfaced circles, but before closing the gap completely, fill with synthetic wadding and insert the end of the wooden handle in order to trap it in the stitching.
4 On each of the two small strips of fabric, fold 1cm (⅜in) to the wrong side all round. Press the strips and then stitch the seams with slip stitch.
5 On each of the six 4cm (1½in) circles of fabric (including the two orange ones) fold 5mm (¼in) to the wrong side all round. Work running stitch close to the edge, as in step 2; gather up each ball, fill with wadding and then close the gap completely and fasten off.
6 Sew the fabric balls and bells to the two fabric ties. Fold each tie asymmetrically, then sew one on to each side of the rattle.

TIP
THE RATTLE IN THE PHOTOGRAPH HAS GATHERED ENDS RATHER THAN THE SIMPLER FLAT ENDS DESCRIBED IN THE INSTRUCTIONS. IF YOU WOULD LIKE TO MAKE GATHERED ENDS, INSTEAD OF THE LARGE FABRIC CIRCLES AND THE INTERFACING CIRCLES CUT TWO 8 × 24CM (3¼ × 9½IN) STRIPS OF FABRIC AND FUSE BONDABLE WEBBING TO THE BACK OF EACH ONE TO PREVENT FRAYING. JOIN THE SHORT ENDS OF EACH STRIP, RIGHT SIDES TOGETHER, TAKING A 1CM (⅜IN) SEAM ALLOWANCE, TO FORM TWO RINGS, AND PRESS THE SEAMS OPEN. JOIN ONE RING OF FABRIC TO EACH SIDE OF THE EMBROIDERY AS IN STEP 3. WORK RUNNING STITCH AROUND THE FREE EDGE OF EACH RING AND GATHER TIGHTLY TO CLOSE THE GAP; FASTEN OFF SECURELY.

❋ Book cover

Size when closed:
18 × 23cm (7 × 9in)
Materials:
15 × 20cm (6 × 7¾in) piece of 28-count (11 threads/cm) ivory linen, DMC ref. 3865
• 8 × 30cm (3¼ × 11¾in) piece of baby pink linen • 48 × 30cm (19 × 11¾in) piece of
Liberty Tana Lawn (Haxby) • DMC Special Mouliné stranded cotton: 1 skein of
each colour listed in the chart key • 10 × 15cm (4 × 6in) rectangle of stiff interfacing
• 48 × 30cm (19 × 11¾in) rectangle of fusible webbing (Bondaweb) • two 20cm
(7¾in) lengths of 1.25cm (½in) pink velvet ribbon • sewing thread to match the
fabric • sewing kit • fabric marker pen.
Refer to the chart on page 74 and the pattern on page 91.

EMBROIDERY

Embroider the motif in the centre of the linen, working each
stitch over two linen threads. Use two strands of Special Mouliné
cotton for the cross stitch and one strand for the backstitch.

SEWING

1 Fuse the webbing to the wrong side of the fabric.

2 Fold 1cm (⅜in) to the wrong side along both long edges of the
   pink linen; press. Centre the strip obtained on the right side of
   the fabric, pin, then attach with slip stitch (this will be the
   spine of the cover).

3 Fold 1cm (⅜in) to the wrong side along both short edges of the
   fabric; press. Fold 3.5cm (1½in) to the wrong side along both
   long edges of the fabric and hem. Fold 5cm (2in) to the wrong
   side of the fabric along each short edge to make the pockets
   that will hold the cover of your book. Secure the pockets at
   each end with slip stitch.

4 Cut out an oval of stiff interface using the pattern. Centre it on
   the wrong side of the embroidered linen, using the
   transparency of the material to help you and then pin it in
   place. Trim the linen 2cm (¾in) from the interfacing all round.

5 Using a double length of thread, work running stitch all round
   the fabric margin. Pull the thread to gather the linen down
   over the interfacing, then fasten off. Sew the linen overlap to
   the interfacing with large slip stitches, taking care not to go
   through to the right side of the embroidery.

6 Pin the oval to the cover 1.5cm (⅜in) from the right side and
   lower edge, then fix in place with invisible stitches.

7 Fold the ends of the ribbon over in a double 5mm (¼in) hem
   and stitch in place. Sew a ribbon halfway down the front edge
   of the cover on each end so you can tie the cover closed.

TIP
THE EMBROIDERED OVAL CAN BE ATTACHED TO THE FRONT OF A READY-MADE
PHOTO ALBUM OR JOURNAL — USE DOUBLE-SIDED TAPE OR MULTI-PURPOSE
GLUE TO SECURE IT. IT WOULD ALSO MAKE A PRETTY FRAMED PICTURE.

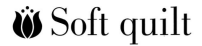 # Soft quilt

Size:
60 × 80cm (23½ × 31½in)
Materials:
28-count (11 threads/cm) Ivory linen, DMC ref. 3865: two 20cm (7¾in) squares, four 15cm (6in) squares and four 9cm (3½in) squares • two 62 × 82cm (24½ × 32¼in) rectangles of pink linen • salmon pink linen: one 15cm (6in) square, one 14cm (5½in) square and one 10cm (4in) square • 8cm (3¼in) square of taupe linen • 62 × 27cm (24½ × 10¾in) rectangle of Liberty Tana Lawn (Haxby) • DMC Special Mouliné stranded cotton: 1 skein of each colour given in the chart key • DMC Pearl Cotton: 1 skein of baby pink and ivory • 60 × 80cm (23½ × 31½in) rectangle of wadding (batting) • fusible webbing (Bondaweb): two 15cm (6in) squares, four 11cm (4¼in) squares and four 5.5cm (2¼in) squares • sewing thread to match the fabric • sewing kit • fabric marker pen.
Refer to the charts on pages 88–89 and the diagram on page 71.

EMBROIDERY

Embroider a motif at the centre of each square of linen. Each design should be worked on two pieces of linen, appropriately sized. Work each stitch over two linen threads and use two strands of Special Mouliné cotton for both the cross stitch and backstitch.

PATCHWORK

1 Pin the fabric to one of the pink linen rectangles with right sides together so that the side edges align and the fabric is 26cm (10¼in) below the upper edge of the linen. Stitch 1cm (⅜in) from the edge of the fabric, then fold the fabric up to meet the top edge of the linen and press.

2 On each of the embroidered linen squares, fold each edge to the wrong side to obtain two 15cm (6in) squares, four 11cm (4¼in) squares and four 5.5cm (2¼in) squares. Iron the folds. Trim the excess linen 1cm (⅜in) from the folds. Fix a square of fusible webbing to the wrong side of the corresponding linen, under the folds.

3 On the squares of salmon pink and taupe linen, fold each edge to the wrong side by 1cm (⅜in); press.

4 Pin all the patches to the linen/fabric assembly following the diagram on page 71. Attach using large stitches with the pearl cotton.

JOINING

Overlay the patchwork and remaining rectangle of pink linen, right sides together. Stitch all round, taking a 1cm (⅜in) seam allowance but leaving a 15cm (6in) gap in one side. Centre the wadding (batting) and attach to the seam all round. Turn the quilt right side out. Tuck in the seam allowances at the opening and slip stitch closed. Work a line of running stitch 1cm (⅜in) from the edge all round and sew across the quilt 5mm (¼in) from the fabric seam line.

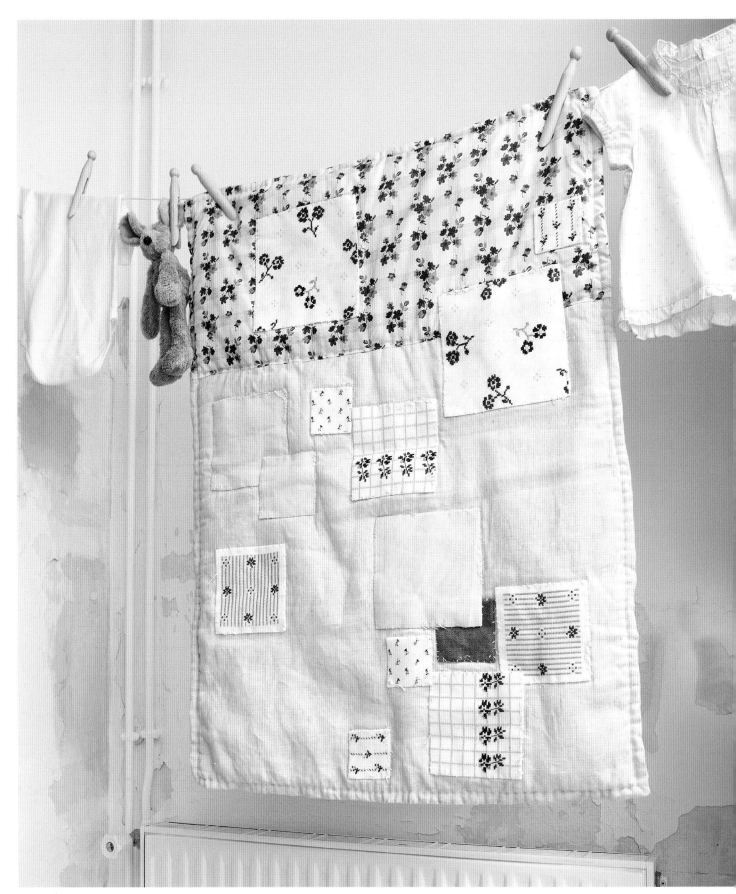

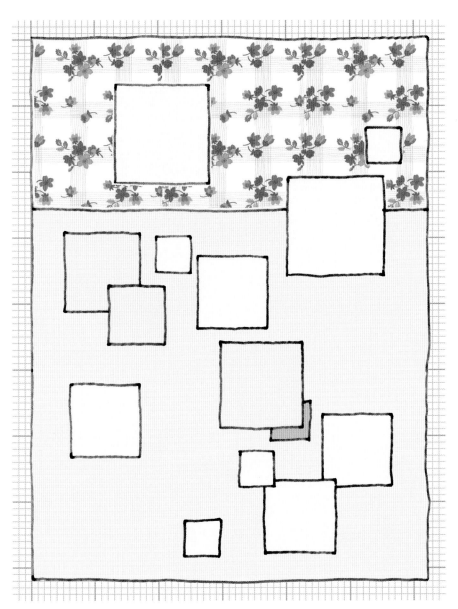

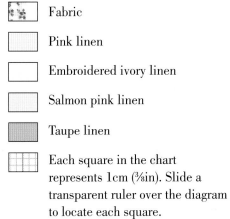

Fabric

Pink linen

Embroidered ivory linen

Salmon pink linen

Taupe linen

Each square in the chart represents 1cm (⅜in). Slide a transparent ruler over the diagram to locate each square.

✳ Cross-stitch charts

Floral bag
Pages 6–9

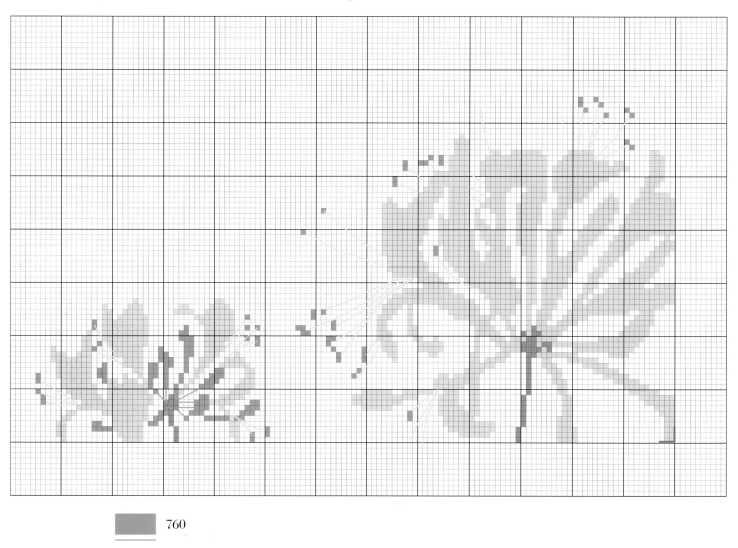

760

598

370

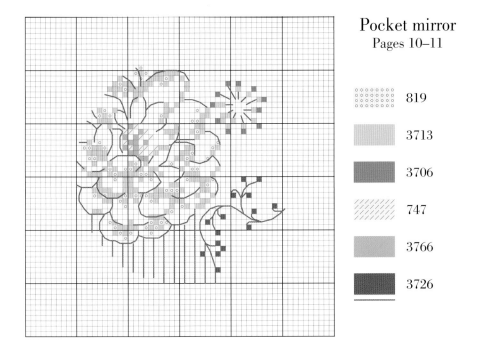

Pocket mirror
Pages 10–11

Little black dress revisited
Pages 22–25

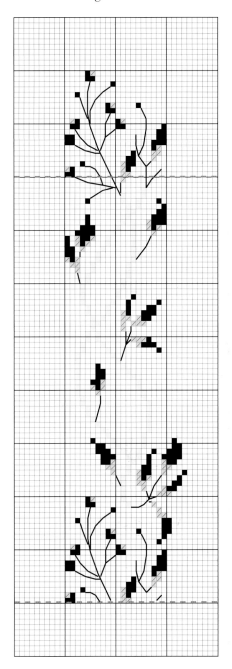

	819
	3713
	3706
	747
	3766
	3726

Hair accessory
Pages 12–13

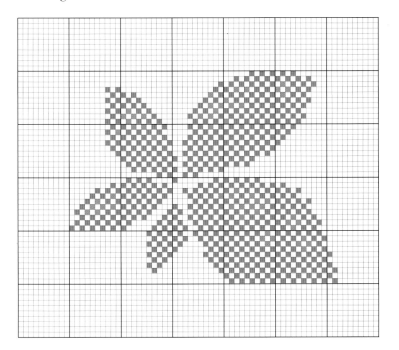

| | 893 |
| | 807 |

 310

 727

 444

73

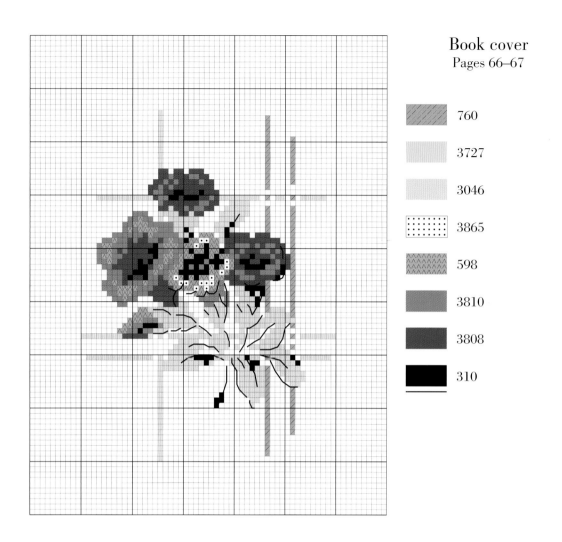

Book cover
Pages 66–67

	760
	3727
	3046
	3865
	598
	3810
	3808
	310

Fancy earrings
Pages 20–21

	3846
	150
	721
	310

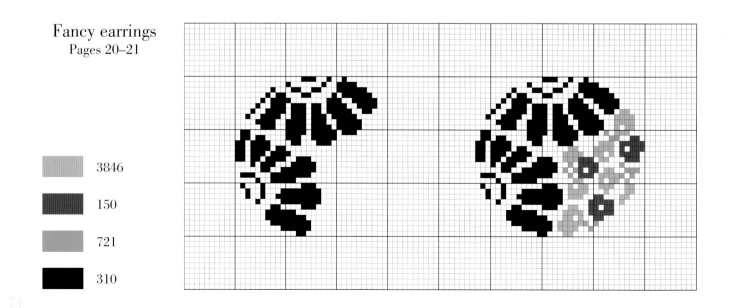

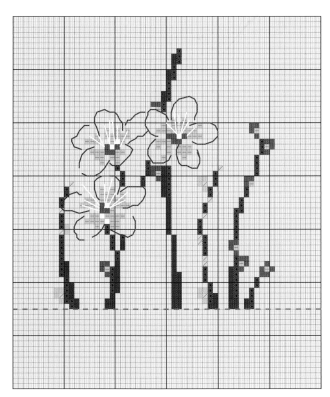

Purse
Pages 16–17

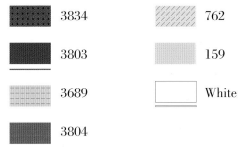

▦	3834		▨	762
▬	3803		▦	159
▦	3689		☐	White
▬	3804			

Backstitch: use one strand of 3803 and two strands of white as indicated.

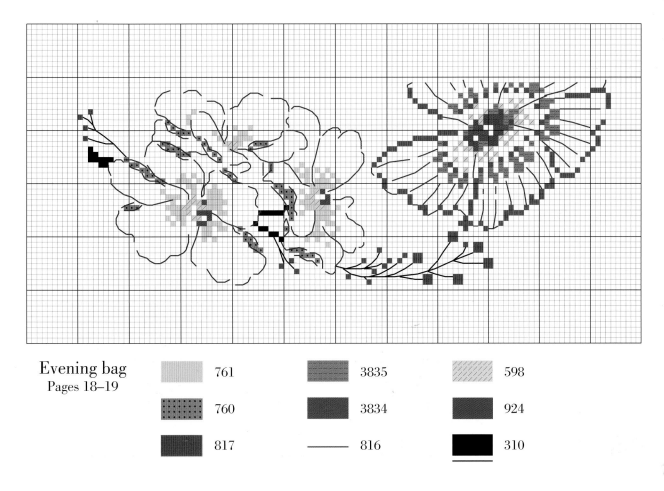

Evening bag
Pages 18–19

▦ 761		▦ 3835		▨ 598
▦ 760		▬ 3834		▬ 924
▬ 817		— 816		■ 310

Photo frames
Corner model
Pages 28–31

 927

926

924

3802

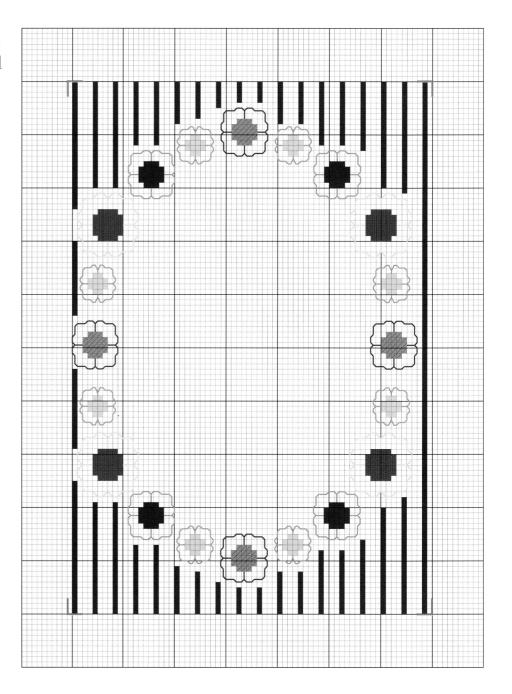

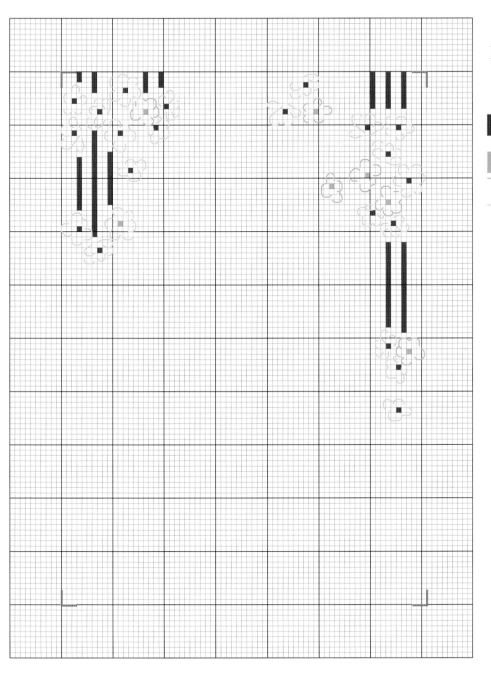

Photo frames
Ruched model
Pages 28–31

3802

316

927

Round cushion
Pages 32–33

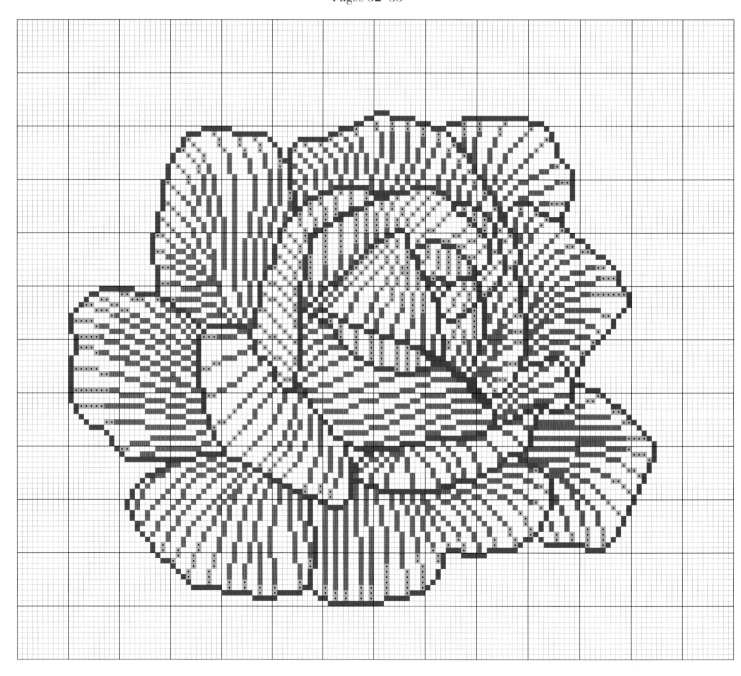

 312

 350

3733

Elegant placemat
Pages 34–35

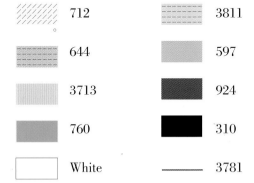

⫽⫽⫽	712	≡≡≡	3811
≡≡≡	644		597
	3713		924
	760		310
☐ White		——	3781

Charming needle case
Pages 38–39

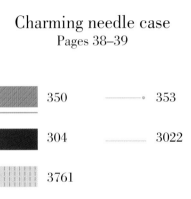

350	353
304	3022
3761	
518	

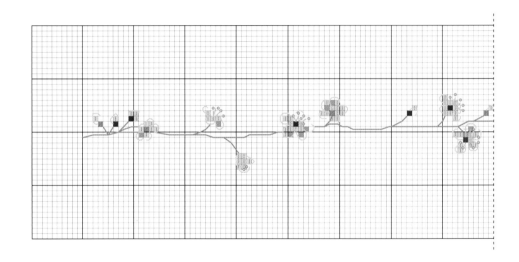

Colourful pot holders
Pages 44–45

3348	
502	
645	

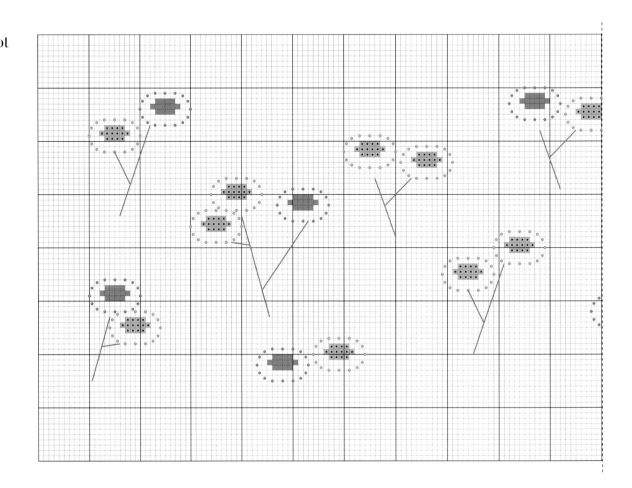

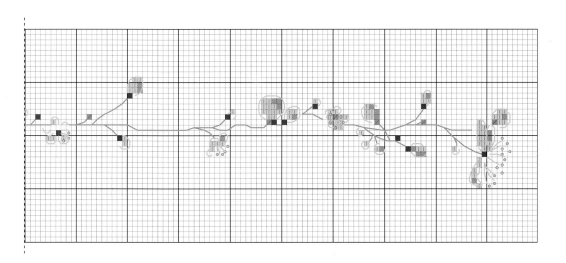

Pretty bow
Pages 14–15

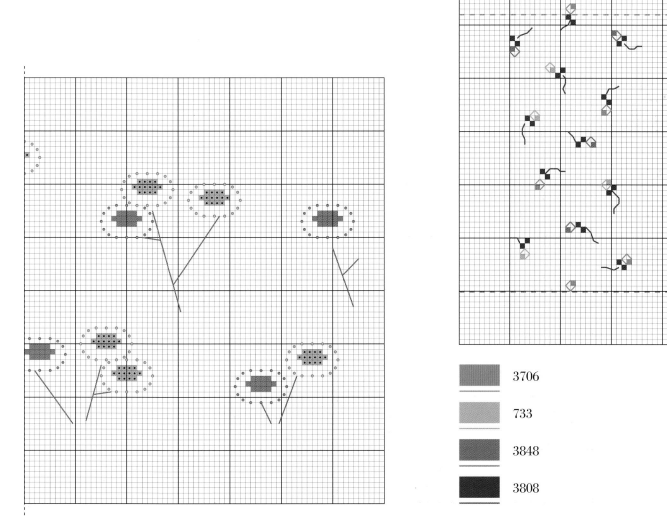

■	3706
■	733
■	3848
■	3808

Colourful pot holders
Pages 44–45

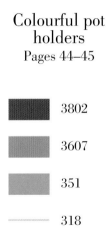

■	3802
■	3607
■	351
—	318

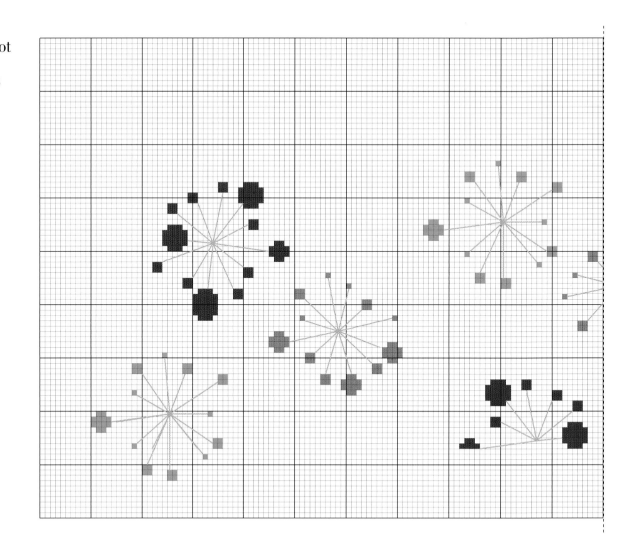

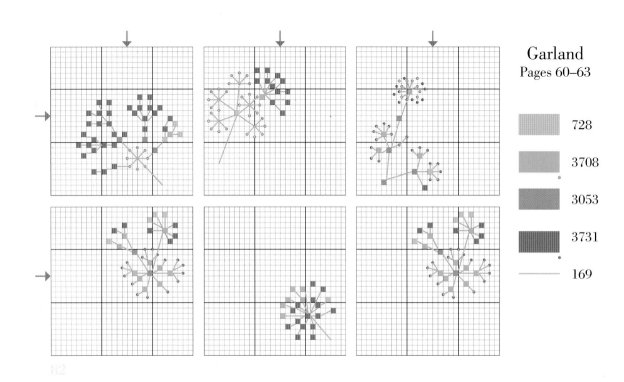

Garland
Pages 60–63

■	728
■	3708
■	3053
■	3731
—	169

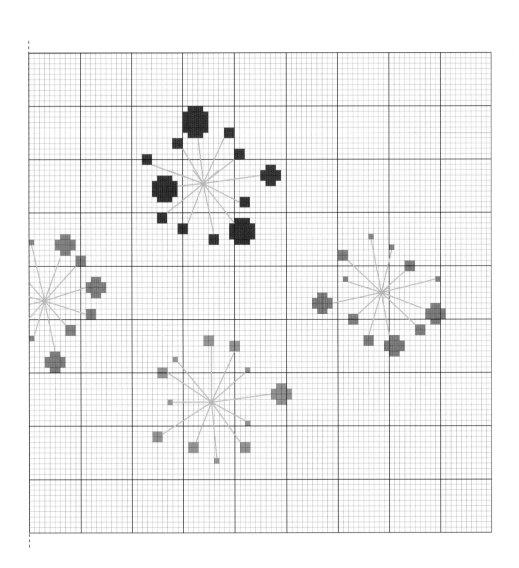

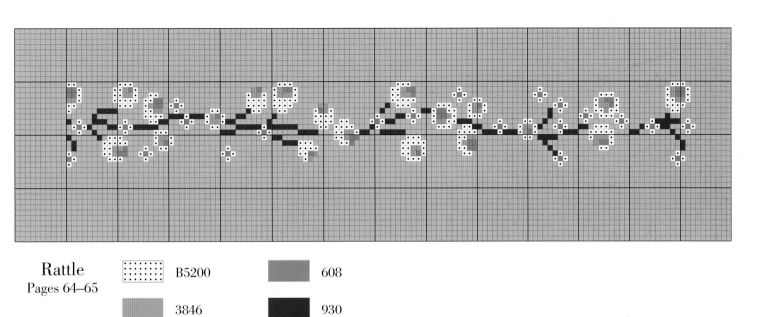

Rattle
Pages 64–65

(B5200 swatch)	B5200	
(608 swatch)	608	
(3846 swatch)	3846	
(930 swatch)	930	

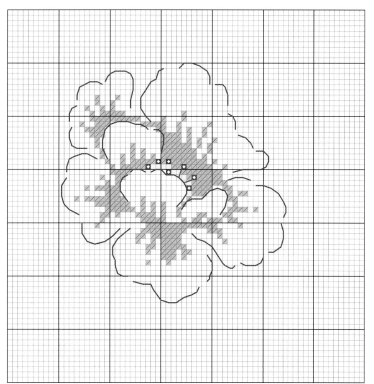

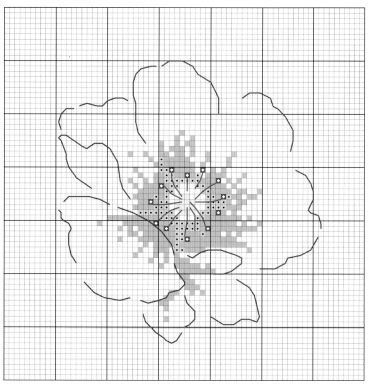

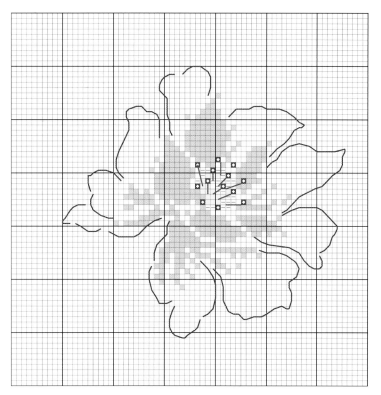

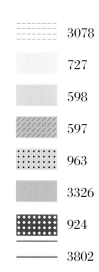

Decorative
stickers
Pages 40–43

-----	3078
▦	727
▦	598
▨	597
▦	963
▦	3326
▦	924
——	3802

Decorative stickers
Pages 40–43

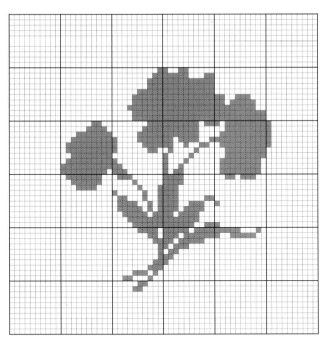

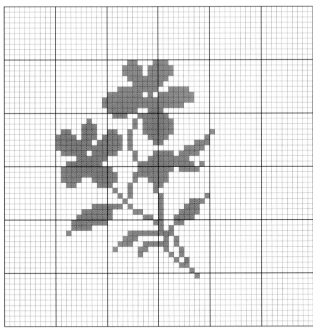

3768

Tea pouch
Pages 36–37

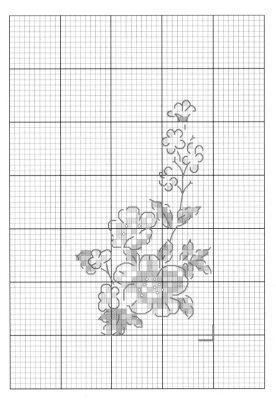

⠿	B5200	——	893 (little flowers)
	712	——	3790 (two large flowers in the centre)
	644	——	3328
	3078		
	3348		
	3817		

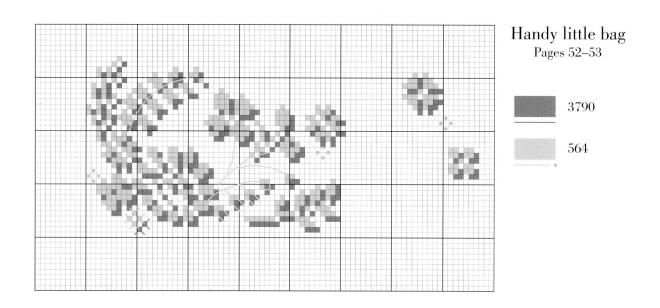

Handy little bag
Pages 52–53

▇	3790
▨	564

Soft bricks
Pages 54–57

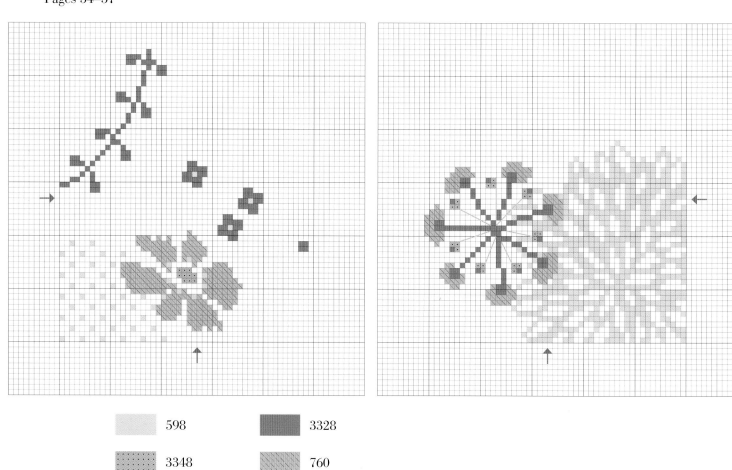

▨	598	▇	3328
▨	3348	▨	760

Box of secrets
Pages 46–47

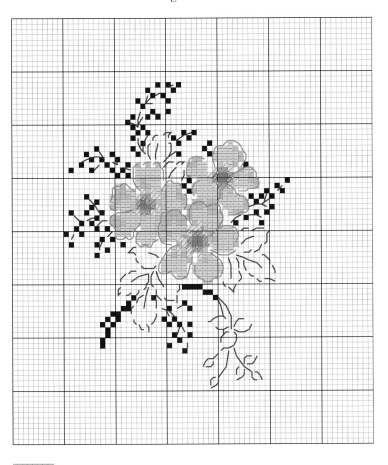

352	
351	
3811	
598	
644	
3023	
3021	
964	
3022	

Bottle holder
Pages 58–59

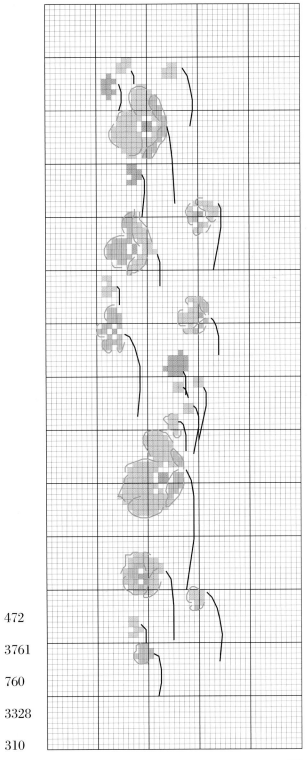

472	
3761	
760	
3328	
310	

Soft quilt
Pages 68–71

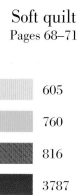

	605
	760
	816
	3787

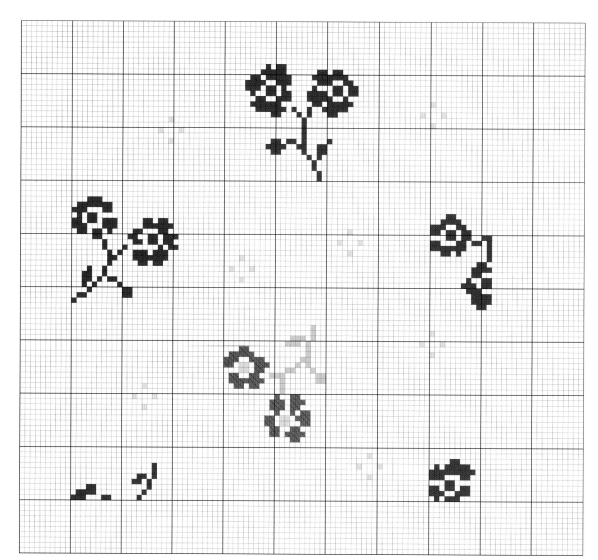

Little slippers
Pages 50–51

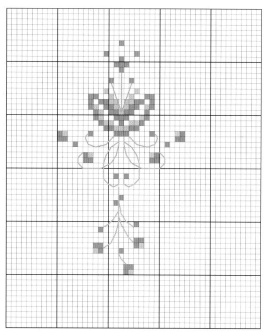

	351
	3752
	932

Soft quilt
Pages 68–71

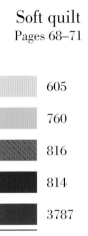

▨	605
▨	760
▨	816
■	814
■	3787
⎯	817

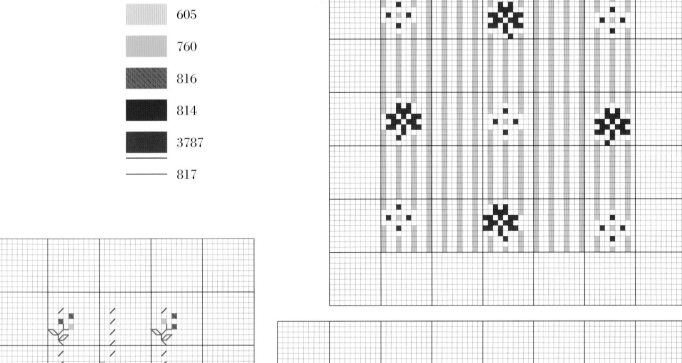

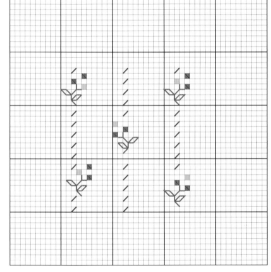

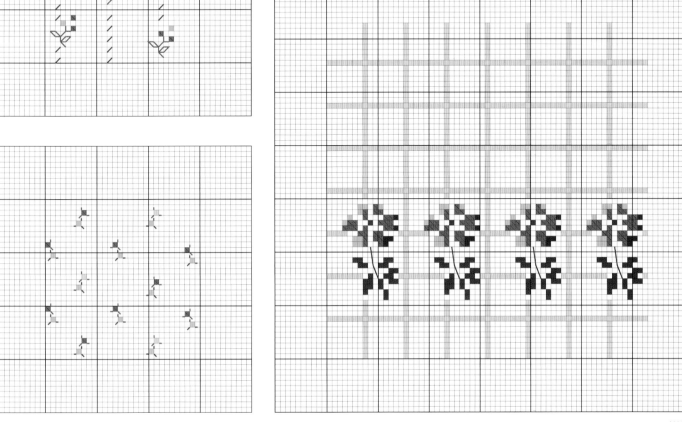

❋ Patterns

USING THE PATTERNS
All the patterns are actual size. Only add a seam allowance if
instructed to do so.
Sometimes a pattern represents only half (or a quarter) of the
shape. In this case, place on the fabric folded in two (or in
four), aligning the broken lines on the fold of the fabric.

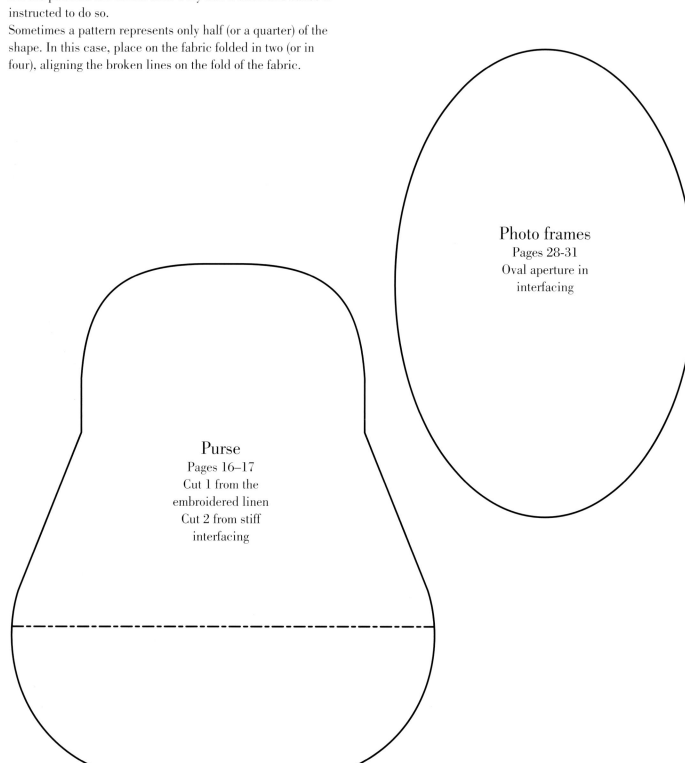

Photo frames
Pages 28-31
Oval aperture in
interfacing

Purse
Pages 16–17
Cut 1 from the
embroidered linen
Cut 2 from stiff
interfacing

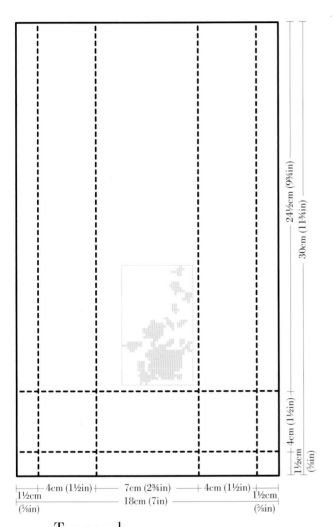

24½cm (9¾in)

30cm (11¾in)

4cm (1½in)

1½cm (⅝in)

1½cm (⅝in) — 4cm (1½in) — 7cm (2¾in) — 4cm (1½in) — 1½cm (⅝in)

18cm (7in)

Tea pouch
Pages 36–37
Folding diagram

Book cover
Pages 66–67
Cut 1 from stiff interfacing

Round cushion
Pages 32–33
Joining diagram

 Fabric A

 Fabric B

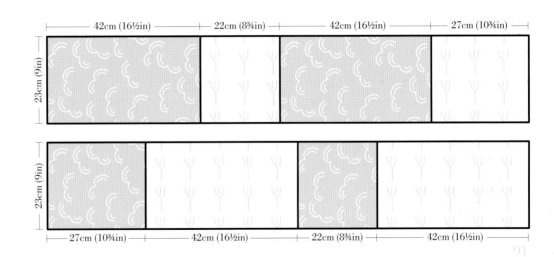

42cm (16½in) — 22cm (8¾in) — 42cm (16½in) — 27cm (10¾in)

23cm (9in)

23cm (9in)

27cm (10¾in) — 42cm (16½in) — 22cm (8¾in) — 42cm (16½in)

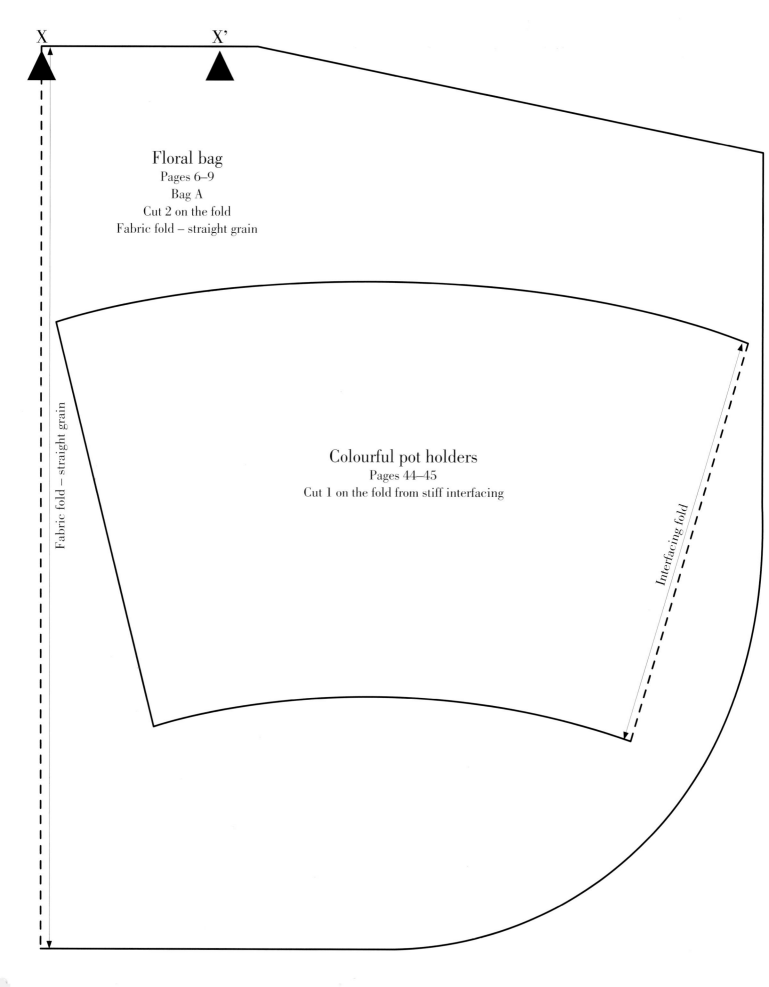

X   X'

Floral bag
Pages 6–9
Bag A
Cut 2 on the fold
Fabric fold – straight grain

Fabric fold – straight grain

Colourful pot holders
Pages 44–45
Cut 1 on the fold from stiff interfacing

Interfacing fold

Floral bag
Pages 6–9
Bag lining B
Cut 2 on the fold

Fabric fold – straight grain

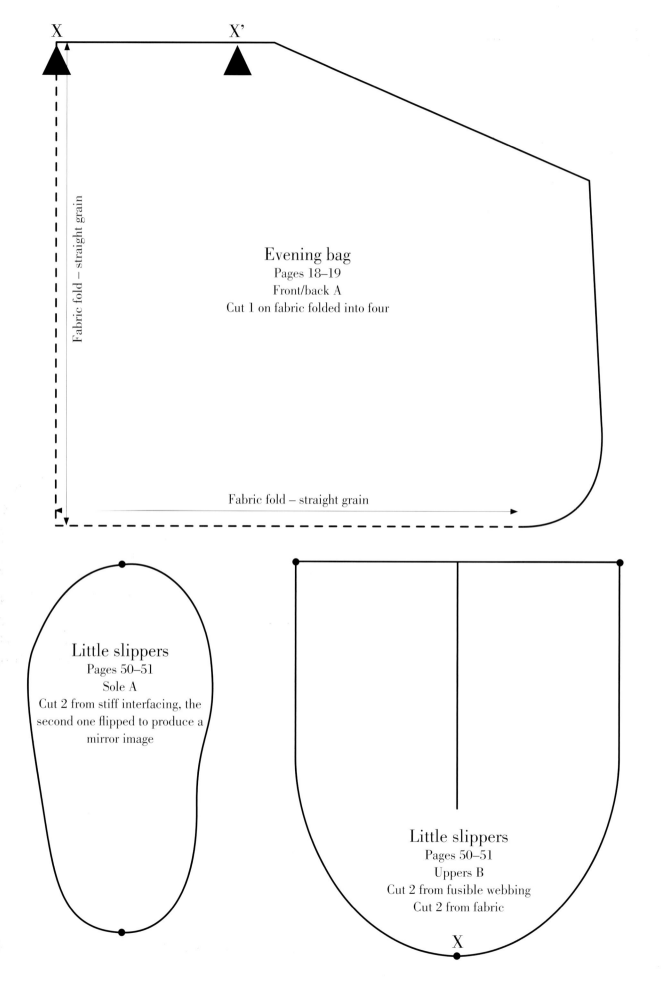

X   X'

Fabric fold – straight grain

Evening bag
Pages 18–19
Front/back A
Cut 1 on fabric folded into four

Fabric fold – straight grain

Little slippers
Pages 50–51
Sole A
Cut 2 from stiff interfacing, the
second one flipped to produce a
mirror image

Little slippers
Pages 50–51
Uppers B
Cut 2 from fusible webbing
Cut 2 from fabric

X

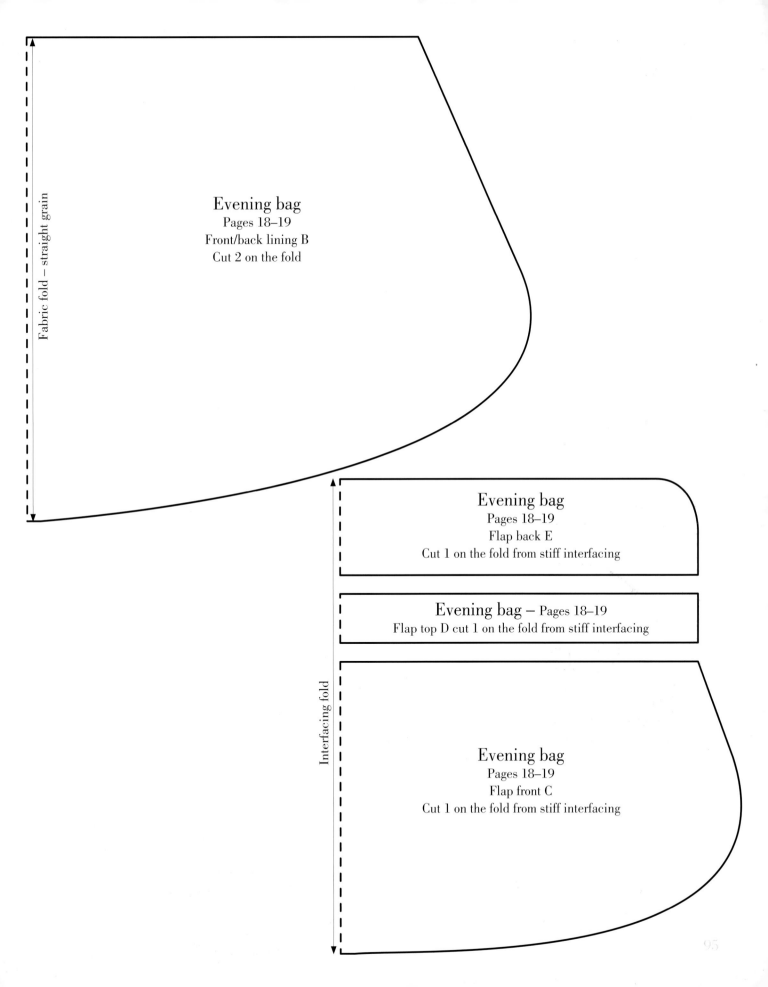

Fabric fold – straight grain

Evening bag
Pages 18–19
Front/back lining B
Cut 2 on the fold

Evening bag
Pages 18–19
Flap back E
Cut 1 on the fold from stiff interfacing

Evening bag – Pages 18–19
Flap top D cut 1 on the fold from stiff interfacing

Interfacing fold

Evening bag
Pages 18–19
Flap front C
Cut 1 on the fold from stiff interfacing

✳ Thanks and acknowledgements

The author would like to thank:
- Stragier, for the Liberty fabrics – http://tissusliberty.blogspot.com
- Psrquilt, for the stiff interfacing and spray adhesive - http://www.psrquilt.fr

The designer would like to thank:
- Loulou Addict – 25, rue Keller 75011 Paris – http://www.loulouaddict.com
- Nanelle – 7, rue Guichard 75016 Paris – http://www.nanelle.fr
- Lin et Cie – 16, rue Bré 75006 Paris – http://www.linetcie.com
- Greengate – http://www.greengate.dk

Thanks also to Florence, Cyril and Ferdinand.

Photography: Fabrice Besse
Design: Sylive Beauregard
Formatting, editing and patterns: Marie Pieroni

First published in Great Britain 2011 by Search Press Limited,
Wellwood, North Farm Road, Tunbridge Wells, Kent TN2 3DR

Originally published in France as Liberty et point de croix
by Fleurus Éditions, Mango Pratique
Copyright © Fleurus Éditions, Mango Pratique, Paris 2010

English translation by Cicero Translations
English edition produced by GreenGate Publishing Services, Tonbridge

ISBN: 978-1-84448-746-2

Suppliers
If you have any difficulty in obtaining any of the materials and equipment mentioned in this book, please visit the Search Press website for details of suppliers: www.searchpress.com

Although every attempt has been made to ensure that the designs used in this book are currently available, some of the fabrics are from Liberty's seasonal range and their continued availability therefore cannot be guaranteed. If you have difficulty in obtaining any of the designs mentioned, the Publishers suggest you choose from the numerous alternative Liberty designs that are available instead.

Printed in China.